Wonders of the Age

درجواب گفت اگر توانم بگویم و الّا زحمت ببرم

چون عارض تو ماه نباشد روشن　　مانند رخت گل نبود در گلشن

مژگانت همی گذر کند از جوشن　　مانند سنان گیو در جنگ پشن

ایشان کیفیت جنگ گیو و پشن پرسیدند　تقریری خوش کرد چنانچه مجموع فضل او را مسلّم داشتند بمصاحبت و مباحثت باین طایفه

مستأنس شد　و شعرا او را امتحانات میکردند و هر لحظه بدیهه و لطیفه دیگر درمیان می آوردند　و فردوسی در فن بدیهه بغایت چابک سوار بود

چو گشتی باسب بدیهه سوار　　برآوردی از خیل فکرت دمار

برمح سخن در صف ارتجال　　شکستی بیک حمله قلب رجال

و چون شعرای غزنین ارتقای ابوالقاسم بر مدارج فنون هنر معلوم کردند　راه مداخلت مجلس سلطان و طرق معرفت او باحجاب آستان

مسدود و مهمل داشتند تا او را با ماهک که از ندمای مجلس سلطان بود ملاقات افتاد و حبل الفت و رشته مودت بهم رسید و محکم گردانید

WONDERS OF THE AGE

Masterpieces of Early Safavid Painting, 1501 – 1576

STUART CARY WELCH

with contributions by Sheila R. Canby & Nora Titley

British Library, London, August 10, 1979 – October 28, 1979

National Gallery of Art, Washington, D. C., December 16, 1979 – March 2, 1980

Fogg Art Museum, Cambridge, Massachusetts, March 20, 1980 – May 18, 1980

FOGG ART MUSEUM, HARVARD UNIVERSITY

On the cover: Detail of *Court of the Gayumars,* no. 8

Frontispiece: *Firdawsi Encounters the Court Poets of Ghazna,* no. 4.

The title of the exhibition is taken from Mirza Muhammad Haydar Dughlat's treatise on the Herat school of painters. He spoke of the artist 'Mawlana Mirak Naqqash as "One of the wonders [marvels] of the age." See Binyon, Wilkinson, and Gray, *Persian Miniature Painting,* p. 190.

This publication was supported by a grant from the National Endowment for the Arts, Washington, D.C., a Federal agency, and by Mr. John Goelet.

PHOTOGRAPHY CREDITS
Nos. 5, 6, 7, 11, 12, 13, 15, 16, 17, 18, 19, 20, 21, 24, 26, 27, 32, 35, 36, 38 by Frank White; no. 74, E. B. Crocker Gallery; nos. 67, 68, 70, 78, 79, by Michael Nedzweski and Barry Donahue, Fogg Art Museum; nos. 3, 5, 6, 8, 10, 15, 20, 21, 24, 26, 27, 29, 30, 32, 35, 36, 38 The Pierpont Morgan Library; nos. 45, 69, 71, 77, 82, 83, 85 courtesy the Museum of Fine Arts, Boston. Others as noted in entries and captions.

LIBRARY OF CONGRESS CARD CATALOGUE NUMBER: 79–2480

PRINTED IN THE UNITED STATES OF AMERICA

Lenders to the Exhibition

Edwin Binney, 3rd

British Library

British Museum

Cleveland Museum of Art

Fogg Art Museum

Arthur A. Houghton, Jr.

Metropolitan Museum of Art

Museum of Fine Arts, Boston

Musée Guimet

Musée du Louvre

Private Collections

Royal Scottish Museum

University Library of Uppsala

Detail of no. 9.

Table of Contents

Foreword

INCREASING NUMBERS of Western museum visitors are becoming aware of the splendors of non-Western art. Today, a moderately educated eye appreciates Chinese painting, recognizes the dignified power of African sculpture and the sensitive elegance of Eskimo ivories. Many, though still too few, realize that great artists were at work in Safavid Tabriz as well.

Wonders of the Age brings together a superb collection of exquisite miniatures, presenting a comprehensive view of painting in the years from the beginning of the sixteenth century until the death of Shah Tahmasp in 1576. The exhibition represents probably the greatest assemblage of sixteenth-century Iranian painting seen together in four hundred years and includes some of the finest Persian miniatures ever created.

This exhibition owes its existence to the cooperation of many individuals and institutions. Our warmest thanks go to Stuart Cary Welch, Curator of Muslim and Hindu Painting at the Fogg Art Museum, for his role in conceiving and selecting the exhibition and writing the catalogue. The generosity of the lenders has also made this extraordinary event a reality. We are extremely grateful to Arthur A. Houghton, Jr., who has agreed to lend miniatures from the beautiful BOOK OF KINGS, as well as to The Metropolitan Museum of Art, which has contributed several of its pictures from this same volume. Several private collectors who also acquired paintings from this manuscript have kindly allowed their treasures to be shown. In addition, one of our host institutions, the British Library, has graciously permitted us on this occasion to show the fourteen miniatures from its renowned QUINTET of Nizami as separate works.

Although the core of the exhibition consists of Shah Tahmasp's BOOK OF KINGS and QUINTET, miniatures and drawings from other sources have also been included to enrich and amplify our appreciation of Safavid court painting. For the earlier years, we are especially fortunate in having been allowed to borrow the manuscript of 'Asafi's *Jamal u Jalal* from the Uppsala University Library as well as a dazzling miniature from the British Museum attributable to Sultan-Muhammad. For loans of works from the later period, our special thanks must go to the Musée du Louvre, the Museum of Fine Arts, Boston, and The Cleveland Museum of Art. We are also particularly grateful to the Musée Guimet, and to Edwin Binney, 3rd, for contributing works by Mir Sayyid-'Ali, one of the founders of the Mughal school, and to the Royal Scottish Museum for lending one of the miniatures separated from the British Library QUINTET. In addition we wish to acknowledge the generosity of several anonymous private lenders.

Recent scholarship has added greatly to our knowledge of this field. The study prepared by Mr. Welch and Professor Martin Bernard Dickson of Princeton University, *The*

Houghton Shahnameh, soon to be published by Harvard University Press, surveys the entire field of early Safavid court painting. For it, Professor Dickson re-examined and re-translated virtually all of the relevant literature, including many contemporary chronicles, memoirs, and diaries, excerpts of which he has generously allowed us to include here.

We would also like to thank all those devoted members of the staffs of the participating museums whose efforts in arranging for, mounting and exhibiting these treasures, and publishing this catalogue are deeply appreciated.

Those of us on the western side of the Atlantic would also like to extend our thanks for the financial support of the National Endowment for the Arts, Washington, D.C., a federal agency of the United States Government, and John Goelet. Their generous donations allowed us to uphold our end of this international collaboration.

J. Carter Brown, *Director*
NATIONAL GALLERY OF ART

Sydney Freedberg, *Acting Director*
FOGG ART MUSEUM

D. T. Richnell, *Director General*
BRITISH LIBRARY REFERENCE DIVISION

Dedication & Acknowledgements

TELEPHONE CALLS at five in the morning, horribly demanding questions about the personal habits of sixteenth-century princes, requests for translations of discouragingly long and complicated inscriptions—all these and more have been suffered by my friend and colleague, Martin Bernard Dickson of Princeton University, to whom I wish to dedicate this partial result of our fifteen-year collaboration. To one who spends happy hours peering at exhilarating pictures, Martin Dickson's literary and historical labors are as mysteriously awesome as they are impressive and essential. If I have twisted and garbled, or, more likely, misquoted, his important work, I accept the shame; for without his scholarship our investigation of Shah Tahmasp's and his artists' pictures would have been far less satisfying, enjoyable, and productive.[1]

We are deeply grateful to Arthur A. Houghton, Jr. not only for having accepted our suggestion that he acquire Shah Tahmasp's *Book of Kings* but also for allowing Professor Dickson and myself to publish it, a far lengthier effort than anticipated and one which must have sorely tested Mr. Houghton's patience. During the period of study preceding the actual writing of *The Houghton Shahnameh* many colleagues were particularly helpful and generous. At the Fogg Eric Schroeder and John Rosenfield gave unstinting encouragement and advice. We are greatly indebted to B.W. Robinson, who was not only the first to accept our radical ideas that Safavid painting emerged from Turkman as well as Timurid sources and that Sultan-Muhammad was the painter of *Rustam Sleeping* (no. 2), but who previously had greatly contributed to our education in the field by lending us his copious and excellent notes to the major collections in the British Museum and Bibliothèque Nationale. We are also beholden, in London, to Basil Gray and Ralph Pinder-Wilson, in Leningrad, to Nataly Grek and Anatoli Ivanov, and in New York, to Maurice Dimand and Richard Ettinghausen.

In preparing for the exhibition, we are particularly indebted to Norah Titley for her initial encouragement and painstaking research, editorial work, and many other invaluable contributions in connection with the catalogue, to Jeremiah Losty and M.I. Waley for their devoted help on many levels. We are particularly thankful to Mr. D.T. Richnell for his constant and incisive support as Director General of the British Library Reference Division. From the first, Michael Rogers of the British Museum also lent his lively encouragement and excellent advice. Mlle. Jeannine Auboyer of the Musée Guimet, Norman Tebble of the Royal Scottish Museum, and Thomas Tottie of the Uppsala University Library were also thoughtfully and efficiently helpful, as was Marthe Bernus-Taylor of the Louvre, whose devotion to the cause deserves special recognition.

Among U.S. private collectors, we are beholden particularly to Arthur A. Houghton, Jr. and Edwin Binney, 3rd for their constant generous cooperation. We are also grateful to

Philippe de Montebello and Dr. Richard Ettinghausen of the Metropolitan Museum of Art, to Jan Fontein and Joyce Paulson of the Boston Museum of Fine Arts, and to Sherman Lee and Stanley Czuma of The Cleveland Museum of Art, without whose generosity in lending miniatures our exhibition would be considerably less significant. Several private collectors, who chose to lend anonymously, have been nobly cooperative and generous in carrying out many dreary but essential chores.

Inasmuch as the Fogg has been responsible for much of the organization of this exhibition and for its catalogue, the Museum's staff has earned our gratitude. Seymour Slive, the Director, and Sydney Freedberg, Acting Director, provided enthusiastic and sympathetic leadership, while Suzannah Doeringer, the Assistant Director, coordinated the extremely complex enterprise. Jane Watts, Registrar, masterfully planned and carried out such intricacies as scheduling, transportation, loan forms, and insurance. Martha Coburn, aided by Carol Mackin, tactfully and effectively kept us within her brilliantly prognosticated budget. Lawrence Doherty foresaw and proposed solutions to security hazards, while Marjorie Cohn ingeniously and devotedly attended to the conservation of the works of art.

For the catalogue we are particularly grateful to Mildred Frost, who organized and brought together the invaluable editorial suggestions of Norah Titley and Sarah Bradley and who also typed much of the manuscript. Sheila Canby not only wrote parts of the catalogue, but also with Glenn Lowry ably carried out a variety of demanding chores. The catalogue was sensitively and effectively designed by Katy Homans. Peter Walsh painstakingly and effectively supervised the many aspects of its production. We are also thankful to Francis W. Canzano, Jr., Jackie McLaughlin, and Robert Savigni of the Acme Printing Company for their dedication to an unusually challenging project.

We are deeply indebted to Mrs. Eric Schroeder and to John Goelet for their generous encouragement of our department not only at the time of this exhibition but also over many years.

At Harvard I am especially beholden to Annemarie Schimmel, Wheeler Thackston, and Peter Heath, who have never failed in giving prompt, accurate, and sympathetic answers to difficult questions in their particular fields.

S. C. W.

1. Throughout this catalogue we have used extracts from many of Martin B. Dickson's new translations from such sources as Dust-Muhammad's *Preface*, the *Book of Kings*, the *Divan* of Hafiz, and many other Persian texts.

Introduction

THE MEREST GLANCE at the paintings assembled here reveals several remarkable characteristics. Their jeweled richness of color evokes the radiance of nature, as in precious stones or the plumage of birds. Their fineness of scale defies our eyesight, and they illuminate an ideal world, shadowless and mostly flat, all elements of which are heightened to the level of fantasy. Many of the pictures stun at fifty paces, but they also invite close, lingering inspection of each tiny configuration, from the lively, often comical heroes, nobles, and demons, to the fabulous animals and birds, ornament, and landscapes.

These miniatures exemplify high court art. Their patrons and artists were supremely civilized. Most were poets, musicians, and calligraphers, as well as men of the world, who intrigued, fought, and loved. They were also devout Muslims and many were mystics. Sultan-Muhammad, who painted *The Court of Gayumars* (no. 8), *Allegory of Drunkenness* (no. 44), and *The Ascent of the Prophet* (no. 63), impresses us as a painter-saint. His somewhat younger colleague in the royal workshop, Aqa-Mirak, a close companion of their patron, Shah Tahmasp, must also have been mystically oriented, as can be seen by his *Faridun Tests His Sons* (no. 14) and *Nushirvan Listening to the Owls* (no. 50), both redolent of Sufi inspiration. By exploring every nook and cranny of these infinitely complex little paintings, viewers will find what they seek, or deserve, whether it be a superbly designed textile, an outrageously funny demon, or a vision of paradise.

All the pictures here share certain characteristics. All are of royal origin, from the courts of the Shahs and princes of the Safavid dynasty; all were painted by major court artists during the first three quarters of the sixteenth century. Technically, they were drawn on paper with reed pens or brushes, after which most were colored in opaque watercolor (or gouache), using glues or gum arabic as binding media, a technique of deceptive simplicity that took years of apprenticeship to master. Pigments were varied, and their manufacture was part of each artist's training, along with making brushes of squirrel or kitten hairs set in bird quills and perfectly fitted to the artist's grip. Some pigments were made by "secret" chemical processes; a few were prepared from such natural ingredients as crushed insects; and others, including the precious mineral lapis lazuli, used to produce the costliest and bluest of blues, had to be powdered and sorted grain by grain. Metals, too, were employed. Silver and gold were pounded between sheets of parchment into thin foils, before being worked in a mortar with rock salt, which was later washed out, leaving the pure metallic pigments. For a warm gold, copper was added; for a cooler one, silver. Copper also provided verdigris, a corrosive green that was often painted on over a protective coating lest it eat through the paper. Applied in large areas as skies, gold was also brushed on in decorative arabesques. Later, it could be tooled or pricked with a stylus for glittering highlights. Miniatures such as those shown here were traditionally included in books or albums, where they were protected from damp, insects, and prolonged exposure to light —their worst hazards. Traditional Iranian artists also executed wall paintings, but most of these have been lost due to the impermanence of the buildings they adorned.

Portraits of artists at work show them seated on the ground, with drawing boards propped on their knees, surrounded by little shells of pigments and binding medium, pens, brushes, and other tools of the trade. The miniature or drawing was fastened to the board for steadiness. Disciplined control not only of wrist and fingers but of the entire body must have been necessary to make the rhythmic, calligraphic strokes so essential to the art.

One wonders what occupational disorders resulted from the excessively long hours spent in such cramped and strenuous positions! For it is obvious that all of the paintings here required a great many hours of toil, if not months or years. We assume that *The Court of Gayumars*, Sultan-Muhammad's most sustained work, was sporadically in progress over a period of years; while his *Hushang Slays the Black Div* (no. 9), the very next folio in the *Book of Kings*, was joyously dashed off in a matter of a week or so. Evidence of the time required to paint a moderately complex Mughal historical picture in the late sixteenth century was found by Dr. Ellen Smart, who read the artist's inscription saying that it took fifty days to complete.[1]

How did a miniature or drawing of the sort shown here come into being? Few, if any, were created purely for their artist's satisfaction. Rather, they represent the combined efforts and inspiration of patrons as well as painters, each of whom was passionately concerned with pictorial art. Illustrated books were traditional pleasures of royalty and of the few high officials who could afford to maintain ateliers, though, as in the West, a few patrons, including Shah Tahmasp and his father, were particularly concerned with this art. They chose the subjects to be illustrated and guided the artists, thus deserving considerable credit not only for the finished works but also for the development of painters' styles. When Shah Tahmasp commissioned a great manuscript, he set into motion a large corps of craftsmen—specialists in paper (which may have been imported), gilders, illuminators, calligraphers, and binders, as well as artists. All contributed to the project, which demanded lengthy and continuing discussions and preparation. The Shah and the director of the scheme, a major figure such as Sultan-Muhammad, played active roles in laying out the volume, page by page. Together they would have re-examined earlier manuscripts and albums from the Royal Library, searching for inspiring ideas, and with keen perceptiveness, they selected subjects for illustration, assigning them to appropriate artists. During our period, fantastic and demonic scenes often fell to Sultan-Muhammad himself, or to his immediate circle of assistants, whereas romantic or amorous ones were given to Mir Musavvir, another of the three senior masters of the *Book of Kings*. Aqa-Mirak, the third member of the trio, was likely to be held responsible for his specialties: animals, dragons, and court portraits, including those of his friend the Shah.

Like cream rising to the top of milk, artistic talent in Safavid Iran usually reached the Shah's court. Whatever an artist's place of origin, whether Shiraz, Isfahan, or some more provincial center, ability eased his way from a bazaar workshop to a governor's establishment, and thence (perhaps as a human offering from the favor-seeking official) to the summit of the Royal Workshop. Once there, he would have been further trained, in company with the aspiring apprentices already at the capital, such as Mirza-'Ali, son of Sultan-Muhammad, or Mir Musavvir's son, Mir Sayyid-'Ali. Painstakingly, he would have been taught the refinements of composition, the blending and matching of colors, drawing from nature, and copying or tracing from the assemblage of earlier miniatures and sketches in the Royal Library or studios. In all likelihood, his artistic personality was recognized and encouraged. If, like Muzaffar-'Ali (nos. 25, 65), his horses were imbued with vital élan or, like Mir Sayyid-'Ali (nos. 61, 67), he showed genius as a textile designer, these gifts were appreciated and put to use. With luck, his work caught the royal eye, and he was invited to collaborate in one of the Shah's current projects.

Usually, however, young painters were assigned to assist the senior masters before being commissioned to compose original designs. As colorers, they worked in close collaboration with the designers or outliners, at first tinting in backgrounds, and eventually painting more crucial areas. One such apprentice, Mir Sayyid-'Ali, seems to have been so appreciated in this humble capacity that he suffered by being held in such servitude rather than encouraged to create original compositions.

On the whole, Safavid painters' lives must have been happy, tranquil, and secure. Their work was satisfyingly creative, and as members of the royal establishment they were privy to the fascinating activities of the Shah's glittering court. We suppose that they not only received ample salaries but also, for particularly admired work, were given bonuses, ranging from purses of gold to robes of honor, jeweled daggers, such trinkets as Chinese blue and white porcelain, or, on rare occasions, income-yielding villages. The rejection of an artist's work, or worse still the withdrawal of patronage, must have been upsetting, even withering experiences. Men of talent, however, were sure to be welcome at rival courts, such as those of the Ottomans, Uzbeks, or Mughals.

Historically, and artistically, the Safavid dynasty was rooted in earlier traditions. Their immediate predecessors, the Timurids and Turkmans, had replaced the Seljuk Turks and the Khans of the Mongol dynasty. The latter controlled Eastern and Western Iran from about 1050 through the period of weakening Mongol power in the fourteenth century. The Timurid dynasty was founded by Timur (Tamerlane), who traced his descent through a Mongol clan associated with the Jenghizkhanids. Timur's campaigns began in the name of the Mongol rulers and stretched from the Aegean to Moscow, Delhi, and the borders of China. Jenghiz Khan's descendants, though Turkified, took pride in their Mongol origins, as can be seen from the term "Mongol," which was applied to Timur's direct descendants, the Mughals, who ruled in India from 1526 until the last emperor was exiled to Burma by the British in 1858. In terms of painting, the Timurid dynasty produced many major patrons, mostly centered at Herat, such as Shah-Rukh (r. 1397–1447), his son Baysunghur ("The Falcon"), who was in Herat from 1421 to 1433, and Sultan-Husayn Bayqara ("The Eagle"), whose rule at Herat from 1469 to 1506 saw the culmination of Timurid literary and artistic creativity. His enlightened, imaginative patronage inspired one of Iran's greatest painters, the almost legendary Master Bihzad, whose illustrations to a *Bustan* of Sa'di, dated the equivalent of 1488, could be said to mark the classical peak of Iranian painting.[2] Less renowned, but characteristic of Bihzad's style is the *Assault on a Castle*, a stray, unfinished

1. Assault on a Castle.
Bihzad.(?) Fogg Art Museum.

miniature which matches the 1488 pictures in complexity, logical handling of space, sensitivity to the world of appearances, and subtle analysis of character (fig. 1).[3] Although many passages are barely sketched in, others reveal the progressive stages in the making of a miniature. Lively and powerful in conception, the design is brilliantly "nailed" together by a whirlingly patterned shield.

A small, wittily observed drawing of two men, the younger of whom teases the older by moving a wine flask just beyond his reach, can be assigned to Bihzad during the peak years of the Cairo *Bustan* (fig. 2).[4] Surgical in its incisiveness, this humorous little sketch anticipates the sparely calligraphic drawings of such Safavid masters as Shaykh-Muhammad (no. 73) and Aqa-Riza.

2. Temptation with Wine. Bihzad. Fogg Art Museum.

OPPOSITE PAGE: *Court of the Gayumars* (no. 8).

چو آمد ببرج حمل آفتاب
جهان گشت با فر و آیین و آب
بتابید ازان سان ببرج بره
که گیتی جوان شد ازو یکسره
کیومرث چون شد جهان کدخدای
نخستین بکوه اندرون داشت جای
سر تاج و تختش بر آمد ز کوه
پلنگینه پوشید خود با گروه
ازو اندر آمد همی پرورش
که پوشیدنی نو بد و نو خورش

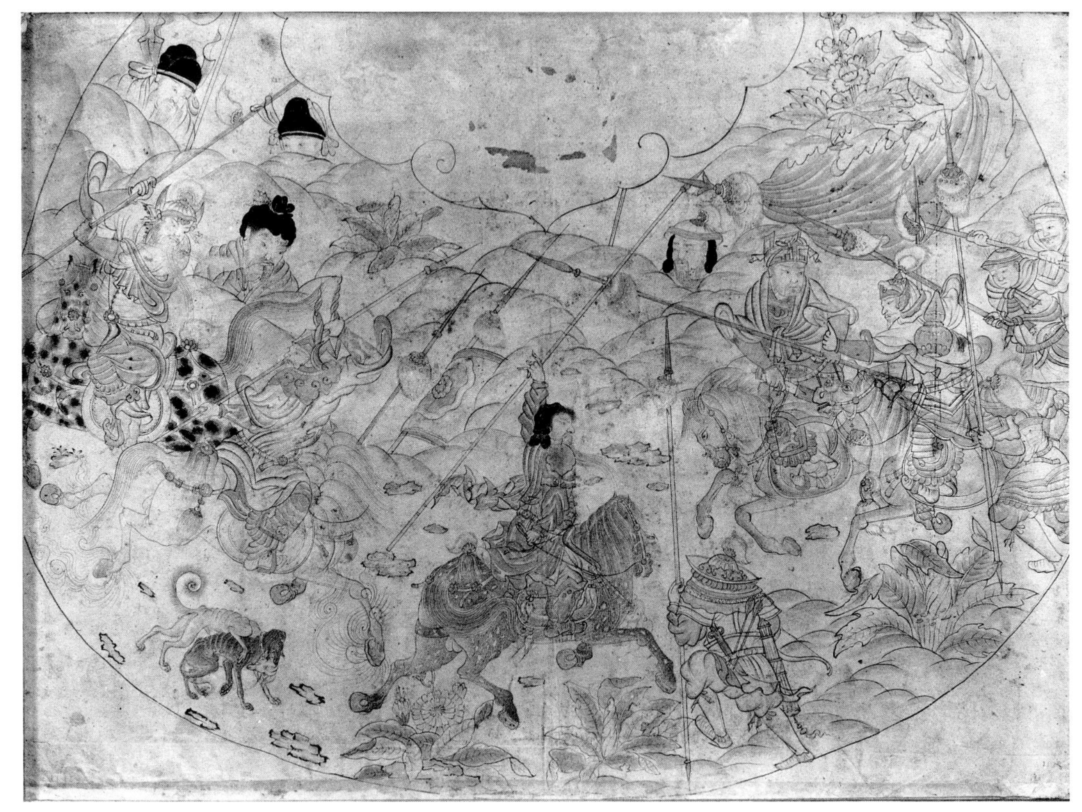

3. Design for a Collar. Museum of Fine Arts, Boston.

While Eastern Iran was controlled by the Timurids prior to the rise of the Safavids, Western Iran was in the hands of the Turkmans, or "west Turks," who established themselves in the central lands of Islam. With the decline of Mongol power in the fourteenth and fifteenth centuries, the Turkmans regrouped into a variety of political formations. Of particular concern to us are the confederacies of tribal clans, such as the rival Black Sheep (Qara Qoyunlu) and White Sheep (Aq Qoyunlu) in eastern Anatolia and Azarbayjan, and the uncommitted clans who were to join the Safavid brotherhood as the Qizilbash and bring Shah Isma'il, the founder of the Safavid state, into power.

The arts of the Black Sheep (who ruled from Tabriz in 1408–1468) and the White Sheep Turkman (at Tabriz in 1469–1501) tend to be more vigorously youthful in spirit and less subtly refined than such Timurid masterpieces as Bihzad's, although they could be described as representative of the Western wing of a single great tradition. Far and away the richest assemblage of Turkman drawing and painting is in the Topkapu Palace Museum of Istanbul.[5] Using this material, it should be possible to trace in detail the development of this supremely vital style, which provided Safavid painting with its earthy might as compared to the Timurid elegance, subtle naturalism, and cerebralism. Animal-like in their energy, Turkman pictures abound in cavorting dragons, demons, birds, and beasts. A design for an embroidered collar in the Boston Museum of Fine Arts (fig. 3),[6] one of the best examples outside of Turkey of Tabriz draftsmanship under the White Sheep dynasty, is boundingly rhythmic and dashing. In this battle scene, figures, vegetation, wraith-like dogs,

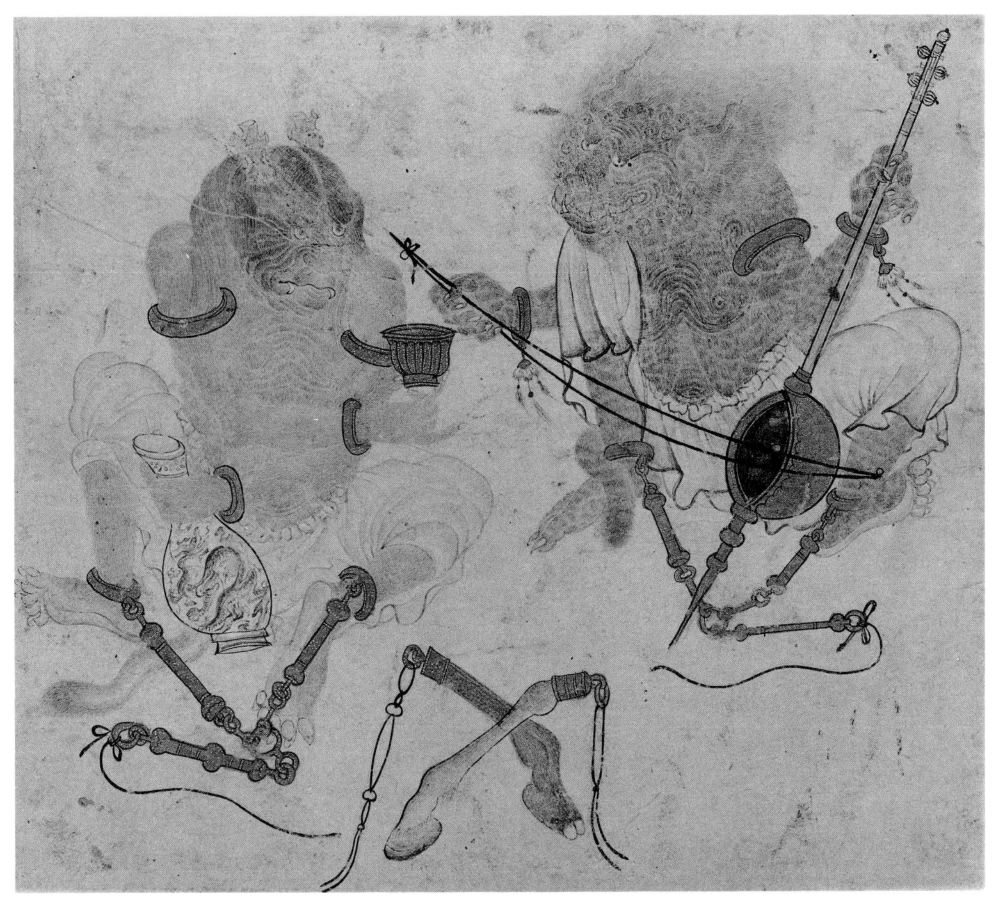

4. Two Fettered Divs. Freer Gallery of Art.

and costumes all point to Chinese sources, and were probably derived from designs on imported porcelains, textiles, and commercial-level pictures—trade items brought from the Orient prior to about 1480, when the Chinese deliberately severed contacts with Iran. A lively drawing of two fettered divs, enriched with colors and gold, now in the Freer Gallery of Art, can be dated to the last decade of White Sheep Turkman rule at Tabriz (fig. 4).[7] Clearly ancestors of Sultan-Muhammad's cavorting divs (see no. 9), these courtly afreets represent Turkman art during its most refined moment, but despite their linear suavity, delicate modelling, and dandified coiffures, one senses danger in their warlockish tendencies.

When, in 1965, we searched for visual proof of the Tabriz Turkman origin of pictures such as figures 1 and 2 in the Topkapu Palace Museum Library, we were rewarded by seeing a manuscript of the *Quintet* of Nizami which had been cited by Professor Zeki Velidi Togan in his *On the Miniatures In Istanbul Libraries* (Istanbul, 1963, p. 25).[8] Although this stunningly attractive volume had been begun for the Timurid Sultan Babur (r. 1449–1457), its calligraphy was completed "at Tabriz" in 1481 by the scribe 'Abd ur-Rahim the Ya'qubi after he had been captured from the Timurids by Pir Budaq of the Black Sheep Turkman and passed in turn to Sultan-Khalil, brother of Ya'qub. The latter commissioned his artists Shaykhi and Dervish-Muhammad to illustrate the volume, which nonetheless was unfinished at the end of his reign. At present, the manuscript contains nine Turkman miniatures and ten Safavid ones, which were added, or in a few instances completed, for Shah Isma'il, the founder of the Safavid dynasty.[9]

5. Bahram Gur in the Yellow Pavilion.
Topkapu Palace Museum, Istanbul.

One of the outstanding Turkman miniatures in this manuscript, dateable to about 1480, is *Bahram Gur in the Yellow Pavilion* (fig. 5), which marks the point of greatest refinement and subtlety in Turkman art, comparable to Bihzad's *Bustan* illustrations of 1488 in Timurid painting, or to the somewhat later *Assault on a Castle* in the Fogg Art Museum (fig. 1). A comparison of the two pictures brings out certain differences between the styles of Western (Turkman) and Eastern (Timurid) Iran during the late fifteenth century, a few decades before the two idioms merged under the Safavids.

Strikingly—almost vulgarly!—rich and vibrant in color, rather than subtly harmonious, the Turkman *Bahram Gur* (fig. 5) is expressionistic rather than naturalistic. Proportions of people and vegetation are as illogical as the treatment of space. The building is flat as a playing card. Bahram Gur and his attendants, although probably intended as portraits of Sultan Ya'qub and his court, are far less individualized than Bihzad's figures. On the other hand, the Turkman mood is passionately lyrical; each tree, flower, sash, or turban seethes with life, and the rocks and clouds carry us into a visionary world next to which Bihzad's seems almost prosaic. Close scrutiny reveals hidden nature-spirits, often grotesque, quite foreign to the orderly ambiance of the late Timurid artist. Despite the absence here of the Freer divs (fig. 4), it is easy to imagine them in this fantastic Turkman setting, which fairly burgeons with the Chinese-inspired peonies and other blossoms found in the Boston collar design (fig. 3).

Fittingly, the peripatetic Istanbul *Quintet* of 1481, with Sultan Ya'qub's marvelously visionary miniatures, fell into the hands of his sister's son, the first Safavid ruler, Shah Isma'il (born 1487, died 1524), whose background and temperament enabled him to appreciate it. This charismatic, inspired leader traced his ancestry to Safi ud-Din, a Sufi Shaykh of Ardabil in Azarbayjan, whose saintliness attracted numerous followers. In about 1300 he founded a dervish order. Under Junayd, a descendant, what had been a purely religious order adopted the militant, extremist forms of the Shi'ite sect, and with the grandfather of the first Safavid Shah, the order or brotherhood turned from mysticism to politics, which led to frequent clashes with the Aq Qoyunlu Turkman rulers centered at Tabriz. In 1499, the twelve year old Isma'il began to organize tribes in Anatolia.

At first, Isma'il was only supported by a few Sufis, but these soon numbered 1500, and before long there were 7000. In 1501 he took Ardabil; then he killed the ruler of Shirvan, and in 1502 Isma'il, the Shaykh of the Sufis, crowned himself Shah, with Shi'ism as the state religion. A year later, he had taken Shiraz, which was rapidly followed by Hamadan, Diarbekr, and Baghdad. Soon the young Shah controlled all of Iran except for formerly Timurid Khurasan, which had been taken by his Uzbek rival, Shaybani Khan. In 1510/11, Shah Isma'il defeated him as well, in a major battle near Merv. The Uzbeks, however, continued to threaten the Safavids from the east, and to the west the Ottoman Turks were equally dangerous, although Sultan Bayazid II congratulated Shah Isma'il upon his early conquests. Later, Sultan Selim massacred Sh'ites in Anatolia, and in the fall of 1514 the Ottoman and Safavid armies fought at Chaldaran, near Tabriz. Victorious, Selim occupied the Safavid capital, Tabriz, where he remained for one week, after which he withdrew, taking with him considerable loot as well as a large number of artisans. Both the Uzbeks and the Ottomans continued to be dangerous neighbors.

Inasmuch as Shah Isma'il was related to the Turkman sultans and grew up within their cultural orbit, it is not surprising that his taste in painting seems to have been more Turkman than Timurid. Such a view is fully consistent with much of his verse, which is fervidly religious and ecstatic, comparable in mood to Turkman painting. Nonetheless, the earliest illustrated manuscript that can be associated with him is a copy of 'Asafi's little-known allegorical romance, *Jalal u Jamal* ("Beauty and Glory," see no. 1 and fig. 6), which contains no miniatures in the Tabriz manner of Shaykhi and Dervish-Muhammad, but rather is painted in a variant of a sub-royal or commercial mode from such centers as Shiraz and Herat. Curiously, this manuscript was copied in Herat itself in the year 1503 by the scribe Sultan-'Ali, presumably Sultan-'Ali of Qayin rather than his better-known namesake of Mashhad. The manuscript contains thirty-four miniatures, a few of which are dated between 1503/04 and 1504/05. Only one of the many illustrations lacks the characteristic Safavid headgear, the renowned *taj*, or "crown," a single-piece skullcap topped with a baton shaped peak, round which the turban was tied. All others, therefore, must have been added for a Safavid patron, almost certainly Shah Isma'il himself.

But how was this possible, inasmuch as the manuscript is from Herat, the Timurid capital until it fell in 1507? We are convinced that although the manuscript was commissioned at Herat for a local patron, and the first (*taj*-less) miniature was painted there for him, the other miniatures (with *taj*) were added after the volume had come into Safavid hands, presumably along with its artists, for the rest of the miniatures are almost identical in style and handling. A likely time and circumstance for its arrival was in May of 1504, when Muhammad-Husayn, one of the rebellious sons of the Timurid Sultan-Husayn Bayqara, joined Shah Isma'il when the latter was campaigning in Mazandaran.

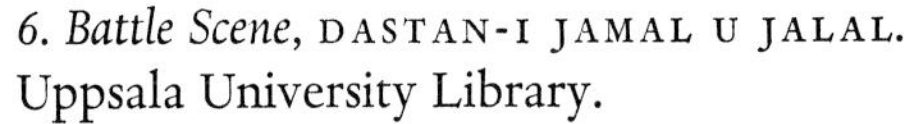
6. *Battle Scene*, DASTAN-I JAMAL U JALAL. Uppsala University Library.

Stylistically, the miniatures in the *Jamal u Jalal* are quite unlike those from Sultan-Husayn's court workshop directed by Bihzad. *A Battle*, for instance, is in a somewhat rough, archaic idiom familiar from the commercial rather than royal levels of Shiraz and Herat (fig. 6). Figures are squat and have rounded, doll-like faces with little individuality; hobby-horse-like mounts also conform to a simple formula; and the background is an all-over pattern of grassy tufts, relieved by occasional folkloristic foliage and flowers.

Of a piece stylistically with the *Jamal u Jalal Battle* is a comparable subject (fig. 7) from a somewhat earlier manuscript, a copy of Ibn Husam's *Khavarannama* ("The Epic of the Eastern Lands"), a popular hagiography recounting the exploits of the saintly 'Ali and his Shi'a (or partisans), written in Quhistan, eastern Iran, a region noted for its populist movements.[10] Although the author completed this text in the year 1426/27, the copy with which

7. *Battle Scene*, KHAVARANNAMA. Present whereabouts unknown.

we are concerned contains miniatures dated 1476/77 and 1487. A few, including figure 7, are signed by "the least of God's servitors, Farhad." In all likelihood, the workshop of the *Khavarannama* was the training ground for the artists of the slightly later *Jamal u Jalal*. But if our two battle scenes (figs. 6 and 7) seem markedly close in style, pictures such as *Dindar Gives Advice* (no. 1) from the Uppsala manuscript are far more intricate and spirited. The figures move more expressively and verge on actual portraiture; and the vegetation, architecture, and sky bring to mind all the ecstatic qualities we find in Shah Isma'il, for whom this miniature must have been painted.

After 1514, Shah Isma'il ceased campaigning and remained at Tabriz. His eldest son, Prince Tahmasp, was born in 1514. Two years later, the prince was sent as titular governor to Herat, where he was educated among the great artists and men of letters of the former Timurid capital, a crucial factor in the development of Safavid art. For while the father encouraged his artists at formerly Turkman Tabriz along the visionary lines already apparent in *Dindar Gives Advice* (no. 1), the infant son was almost literally cutting his teeth on the subtler, more harmonious, and more naturalistic miniatures of the school of Bihzad. Although by now past his prime as a practicing artist, Bihzad remained in Herat during the prince's governorship, and his view of art continued to be influential.

The exhilaratingly vital *Rustam Sleeping While Rakhsh Fights the Lion* (no. 2) argues that Shah Isma'il's enthusiasm for painting was on a par with that of such Turkman predecessors as Sultan Ya'qub as well as of his son, Tahmasp, who has gone down in history as one of Iran's most illustrious patrons. Dynamic as lightning, this illustration to an incompleted *Book of Kings* can be attributed to the great Safavid painter Sultan-Muhammad, most of whose major works are included in this exhibition. Here, cheered on by Shah Isma'il's gusto, he has created a masterpiece of controlled energy that far surpasses his promising, but tentative, works in the Uppsala *Jamal u Jalal*, such as *Dindar Gives Advice*. (no. 1). Furthermore, this picture and a few closely related ones (such as nos. 9 and 10) represent a moment of extraordinary creativity, when the founders of the Safavid state and of its school of art joined forces in perfect collaboration. Sultan-Muhammad's later works, such as the signed *Allegory of Drunkenness* (no. 44), which enables us to attribute the present miniature, and *The Court of Gayumars* (no. 8), however marvelous they may be, are not quite so rapturously energized.

Like time, artistic styles are in constant change; and disappointingly few examples of Sultan-Muhammad's work for Shah Isma'il have survived from the years prior to the return in 1522 of Prince Tahmasp from Herat, another crucial moment in the development of Safavid painting. For the prince's years at the former Timurid capital imbued him with a taste for the tranquil idiom of Bihzad, an idiom totally at odds with the unleashed animality achieved by his father through the wizardry of Sultan-Muhammad. In all likelihood, that great mentor of Apollonian painting, Bihzad, also moved to Tabriz at this time, and if Shah Isma'il's and Sultan-Muhammad's ferocious artistry was able to withstand the onslaught of a princely child, it yielded before Bihzad, the almost legendary personification of art. Like oil poured on raging seas, Timurid tastefulness calmed the surging artistic rhythms of Isma'il's Tabriz.

Energies such as those of Sultan-Muhammad and Shah Isma'il, however, could not be

8. *A Polo Game,* GUY U CHOWGAN. Sultan-Muhammad. State Public Library, Leningrad.

wholly subdued. During the years following Prince Tahmasp's return to Tabriz, the royal ateliers were feverishly productive. Their most ambitious project was the *Book of Kings,* of which a minor portion of the miniatures and illuminations comprise a major part of this exhibition (nos. 3–39). Although the only date in this vast ocean of a manuscript, 1527/28, is found in a miniature on folio 516 verso (no. 30), the volume must have been in progress earlier. We suspect that it was already under way prior to 1522, and that its earliest miniatures, such as *Hushang Slays the Black Div* (no. 9) and *The Death of King Mardas* (no. 10), were painted for Shah Isma'il by Sultan-Muhammad at about the same time as his *Rustam Sleeping,* which we further believe is an unfinished picture for the same project.

Other pictures attributable to the same artist for the *Book of Kings,* such as *Faridun Crosses the River Dijla* (no. 12), can be dated by their similarity to miniatures identical in style in a remarkable pocket-sized manuscript in Leningrad, a copy of 'Arifi's *Guy-o Chowgan* ("The Ball and Mallet") copied in 1524/25 by an artful young scribe, Shah Tahmasp himself![11] Perhaps because his father had died in 1524, the new Shah's taste for the style of Herat is dominant in the miniatures of this manuscript, which can be assigned to the court artists, including the aging Bihzad and the aspiring Shah himself, who was becoming an able artist.[12] *A Polo Game* (fig. 8) is one of several miniatures assignable to Sultan-Muhammad, who here has adjusted, or even disguised, his style to the Bihzadian manner.[13] But beneath the minuscule finish and seeming naturalism, the lively Tabriz master is easily recognized. His ponies twang like released springs, and the players' torsos rise mightily in their saddles, with little apparent concern on the artist's part for correct proportion. As before, the resilient, ever creative, and comical Sultan-Muhammad must have delighted his Shah.

If the boy Shah once had favored Bihzad over Sultan-Muhammad, his view of art was now moderating. Although he may never have developed intense admiration for such pictures as *Rustam Sleeping*, one can be sure that he responded fully to Sultan-Muhammad's creative passion in its new, calmer, and more harmonious form. Sultan-Muhammad had devoted all his intense, wise painterliness to his new master in creating his supreme masterpiece, *The Court of Gayumars* (no. 8), a loving work of many years. In it, he brought together the finesse and subtlety of the Herat tradition and the vigor and earthiness of Tabriz. The painter's fellow artists were "overpowered by this work," as one of them, Dust-Muhammad, stated in his Preface to an album he prepared for Bahram Mirza, a brother of the Shah. Presumably Shah Tahmasp also appreciated it, despite concealed grotesques, Turkman-like expressiveness, and visionary excesses. We suspect that he always preferred more naturalistic and restrained art, despite Sultan-Muhammad's attempts to persuade him otherwise.

As he grew older, Shah Tahmasp's penchant for orthodoxy increased. In 1537, he and his Grand Vazir, Qadi-yi Jahan, stopped at Tehran for the trial and sentencing of extremist Sufis. By now, his own father's poems ("I am God! I am the staff of Moses!") would have been interpreted as raw heresy. In 1541, Shah Tahmasp led a campaign against extremists in Khuzistan. His changes of attitude towards life were reflected in the later pages of his *Book of Kings*. But if, on one hand, his pictures reveal increased rigidity and hard-headedness, on the other they hint of deeper, more sensitive feelings, comparable to the disturbing dreams he wrote about in his *Memoire*. Apparently, Sultan-Muhammad perceived his patron's multi-levelled, often contradictory moods, and interpreted them in such miniatures as *The Death of Zuhhak* (no. 13) in which outward normalcy veils a world as ghoulish as the most extreme fantasies hiding in *The Court of Gayumars* (no. 8). Other worldly elements were lent acceptability by touches of humor and decorousness.

Shah Tahmasp's corps of artists included others no less gifted than Sultan-Muhammad. Infinitely controlled and gentle, with unerring grace as a painter was another senior master, Mir Musavvir, whose greatest work, *The Nightmare of Zuhhak* (no. 11), also contains profound undercurrents. But while Sultan-Muhammad challenges the observer with such passages, they were deeply hidden in tiny rocks or crevices by the Mir.

Aqa-Mirak was another of Shah Tahmasp's major artists, said to have been his closest companion among them. Outwardly courtly and formal, he too plumbed the depths and scaled the heights. The most painterly of the Shah's artists, Aqa-Mirak composed pictures with the confident bravery of heroic Rustam. His *Faridun in the Guise of a Dragon Tests His Sons* (no. 14) is at once a design of the utmost inventiveness and effectiveness, a disarming bestiary, and a microcosm of intriguing earth spirits. Although his horses are of unrivalled elegance, and the dragon's smile captivates, one senses that Aqa-Mirak's personal joy and release came in painting the transparencies of the rocks. We delight, too, in his more vivid but comparable passage from *Bizhan Forces Farud to Flee* (no. 22).

Whether or not the Houghton *Book of Kings* was begun for Shah Isma'il or for his son, most of its 258 miniatures were painted for Shah Tahmasp, and the project went on over a period of many years. So monumental an undertaking required many artists, and we have isolated fifteen distinct hands, most of whom are identifiable by name. Fascinatingly, these artists represent two or more generations: that of Sultan-Muhammad and Mir Musavvir;

that of their sons, Mirza-'Ali and Mir Sayyid-'Ali; and that of the still younger master, Shaykh-Muhammad, whose *Fariburz Against Kalbad* (no. 27) was added to the manuscript in about 1540, a few years after the completion of the project.

Pictures by artists of the second generation, which had grown up in the established court of Shah Tahmasp rather than participating in the exciting formation of Shah Isma'il's new school, reveal distinctive qualities. Although such artists as Mirza-'Ali were aware of the vital Turkman strand in the Safavid style, they were trained in the synthesized Safavid manner that included so many characteristics of Bihzad. Thus, their work seems calmer, more elegantly refined, more cerebral, and less earthy than that of the first generation. Mirza-'Ali's world, as compared to his father's, seems more closed-in, a microcosm of life rather than an all-encompassing vision. If the father created broad characterizations of all human types, the son narrowed his gaze, concentrating upon the elegant, even effete types of his patron's court. Like Mir Sayyid-'Ali, he so lovingly recorded every texture and nuance of shape that his pictures are precise studies of Safavid material culture.[14] By about 1535, such miniatures for the *Book of Kings* were stylistically similar to those for Shah Tahmasp's second great manuscript, the British Library's *Quintet* of 1539 to 1543.

In his Preface to the Bahram Mirza Album of 1544/45, Dust-Muhammad wrote of "Sultan-Muhammad, Aqa-Mirak, and Mir Musavvir, who painted in the Royal Library, and beautifully illustrated a royal *Shahnama* ('Book of Kings') and a *Khamsa* ('Quintet') of Shaykh Nizami." The former is almost certainly the Houghton manuscript, and the latter the *Quintet* in the British Library, from which all the contemporary miniatures are included in this exhibition (nos. 48–65). A more authoritative encomium scarcely could exist, for Dust-Muhammad was not only an eminent connoisseur, a calligrapher, and a distinguished man of letters, but he was also a painter trained by Bihzad. Moreover, he actually participated in the *Book of Kings* project (nos. 31 and 34).

Despite the incomplete state of the British Library *Quintet*, which originally included —or was planned to include—more pictures than the fourteen contemporary ones it now contains, it is clear that Shah Tahmasp intended it to be quite different from the *Book of Kings*. Having become an ever more discriminating connoisseur, he now wanted a volume illustrated solely with masterpieces in the fully synthesized Safavid style of the moment. Old-fashioned or awkward artists were excluded from the new project, which was realistically scheduled for completion within a matter of years rather than decades. One need only handle this majestically unified, technically masterful, impressively compact production of the royal studios to sense that it is the artistic equivalent of the Shah's most effective phase as a ruler, the years when he campaigned against dissidents within the realm and triumphantly protected it from exterior enemies.

Five of the nine major artists known from the *Book of Kings* contributed to the *Quintet* as it now stands, and Dust-Muhammad wrote that Mir Musavvir, whose miniatures for this project must have been lost, also worked on it. Sultan-Muhammad and Aqa-Mirak were joined by Mirza-'Ali, and Mir Sayyid-'Ali, who had been apprentices or very young masters in the years of the *Book of Kings*; and the stylistic uniformity of their miniatures was so marked that until recently some critics have claimed that the individual styles of Shah Tahmasp's artists could not be sorted out!

It could be argued that Safavid painting had now reached its "classic" peak, that the technical and formal perfection and emotional ripeness of the *Quintet* were unsurpassable. Conceivably, Shah Tahmasp felt this way, and instead of urging his artists to strive further or to repeat their successes to the point of boredom, he withdrew his patronage, possibly before the *Quintet* had been completed. Contemporary sources, including the Shah's own *Memoire*, shed light upon his dwindling enthusiasm for painting and other pleasures. He had long been prone to moods of repentance, especially at times of crisis. In 1534, when exterior and interior enemies threatened, he had, in his own words, "wash[ed] away the stains . . . of pulverized emerald [hashish] and liquified ruby [wine]." "Thenceforward," he wrote with pride, "debauchery and licentiousness were suppressed throughout our land." Qadi Ahmad, a calligrapher and man of letters, reveals that his denial of painting in particular occurred in about 1544/45, "when the monarch, having wearied of the field of calligraphy and painting, occupied himself with important affairs of state, with the well-being of the country, and the tranquility of his subjects. . . ." By 1556, his disaffection for painting was so complete that Shah Tahmasp issued an edict of "Sincere Repentance" formally banning the secular arts throughout the realm.

Ironically, the Shah's rejection of painting contributed to the founding of another great Persianate school, that of the Mughals of India. For the second Muhgal emperor, Humayun (r. 1530–40; 1555–56), who had been forced into exile from India, visited the Safavid court at Tabriz in 1544. While there, he invited Mir Musavvir to join his entourage, according to Qadi Ahmad, "but his son, Mir Sayyid-'Ali, was more artful than the father" and hearing of the emperor's interest "rushed off to India, leaving his father to follow." Mir-Sayyid-'Ali's *Young Scribe* (no. 74) and his *Mir Musavvir Offers a Petition* (no. 81) represent this extension of Safavid art at the Mughal court, as does a portrait of Shah Abu'l Ma'ali (no. 75) by Dust-Muhammad, who went uninvited to the Mughal court, apparently to escape Shah Tahmasp's prohibition of wine.

Shah Tahmasp's fickleness towards painting also set in motion an extraordinary chapter of Safavid art. In the very year of the "Sincere Repentance" that ended patronage at his own court, he appointed Sultan Ibrahim Mirza, son of Bahram Mirza, to the governorship of Mashhad. Much admired by the Shah, this nephew was as keen a patron of painting and calligraphy as his uncle had been. When patronage ended at the court of Tabriz, it flourished at Mashhad. In 1556, another major Safavid manuscript was begun for Ibrahim at his capital, a *Haft Awrang* ("The Seven Thrones") of Maulana Nuru'd-din Abdu'r-Rahman Jami, the mystical poet who had lived from 1414 to 1492. Despite the lack of signatures, the twenty-eight miniatures of this manuscript, now in the Freer Gallery of Art, Washington, can be attributed to several of the leading court painters.[15] Although by this time Sultan-Muhammad had died and Dust-Muhammad, Mir Musavvir, 'Abd us-Samad, and Mir Sayyid-'Ali had joined the Mughal court, Aqa-Mirak, Mirza-'Ali, and Muzaffar-'Ali provided pictures for young Sultan Ibrahim's excitingly inventive undertaking. Among its miniatures, we recognize examples by Qadimi, one of the rowdier spirits of the *Book of Kings* (see nos. 17 and 23), whose style had now assumed his notion of courtly graces, as in *Horseman and Groom* (no. 79). 'Abd ul-'Aziz followed a similar course, after having been omitted from the roster of talent for the *Quintet*, possible on behavioral rather than artistic grounds

9. *Yusuf Entertained at Court*, HAFT AWRANG. Shaykh-Muhammad. Freer Gallery of Art.

(see no. 72). But a brilliant younger artist, Shaykh-Muhammad, in some ways outshone all others in the Jami project. His *Fariburz Against Kalbad* (no. 27) was one of a pair of pictures added to the *Book of Kings*, along with *Haftvad and the Worm* (no. 31), signed by his teacher, Dust-Muhammad. Unrepresented in the *Quintet*, Shaykh-Muhammad's artistic personality neatly matched the penchants of Sultan Ibrahim, who spurred him on in quickeningly eccentric paths. Confident of his uncle's devoted loyalty at this time, Ibrahim's appetite for painting was whetted by its illicitness. At the outset, Shaykh-Muhammad's Jami illustrations did not differ markedly in mood from the classical restraint of the *Quintet*. Soon, however, as in *Yusuf Entertained at Court Before His Marriage* (folio 132 recto, fig. 9), new directions were explored. Admired for his portraiture, and known for his "Frankish" (European) manner, Shaykh-Muhammad studied humanity to psychological depths previously seen only in the concealed earth-spirits of Sultan-Muhammad and Aqa-Mirak. If his Yusuf is an idealized portrayal of Ibrahim himself, as we believe, the candid representations of the fat, middle-aged courtiers gazing upon him may also have been drawn from life, with acerbic wit. But this powerful composition should be interpreted on several levels: as a view of the Sultan's Mashhad court; as the illustration to Jami's tale; and in a mystical light, comparable to Sultan-Muhammad's *Allegory of Drunkenness* (no. 44). In the earlier picture, wine is the vehicle to spiritual ecstasy, whereas in Shaykh-Muhammad's miniature it is a "beardless one," a beautiful youth seen as the *shahid* ("witness," for he is the actual witness of divine beauty). To contemplate his face in this form of Sufi meditation, known as *nazar*, is a kind of worship; and adoring him from a distance might induce true ecstasy. This practice was

10. Majnun Eavesdrops on Layla's Camp,
HAFT AWRANG.
Shaykh-Muhammad. Freer Gallery of Art.

considered hazardous, however, as it also provided a noose whereby Satan ensnared mystics. Considering that Shaykh-Muhammad's father was a leading Sufi as well as a famed calligrapher, this interpretation of his son's picture is fully justified.

In compensation for the impossibility of borrowing the Freer Jami, this exhibition includes two portraits by Shaykh-Muhammad which represent his style during the early period of the volume, *Kneeling Youth Reading* and *An Amir Seated Beneath a Tree* (nos. 76 and 77).

Majnun Eavesdrops on Layla's Camp, another picture for the Jami by the same artist, might have outraged the repentant Shah (folio 253 verso, fig. 10). Instilled with the bodily rather than cerebral energy of lower culture, this miniature recalls the vitality and spatial illogic of Sultan-Muhammad's early masterpiece, *Rustam Sleeping* (no. 2), with a few major differences. Powerful forms were coming together implosively in the latter, whereas those in the former seem to be exploding in every direction. Further characteristics, which caused a friend to comment on the Jami's "evil style," are apparent in the twisted humor of the people and animals, though these could also be read as Sufi metaphors. Excess and dissonance increased in Shaykh-Muhammad's paintings, spurred on by his almost demonic patron. His *Puzzling Amir of Bukhara* (no. 80), with its ambiguous characterization, burningly peculiar colors built up over an inky ground, and writhingly organic forms, represents the artist's style during the later years of the *Haft Awrang*.

Even Mirza-'Ali, whose refined courtliness of style enhanced the *Quintet* (see nos. 54, 59), fell under Ibrahim's spell in his miniatures for the Freer manuscript. *Salaman and*

11. Salaman and Absal on the Heavenly Isle, HAFT AWRANG.
Mirza 'Ali. Freer Gallery of Art.

Absal on the Heavenly Isle (folio 191 verso, fig. 11) at once looks back to the artist's *Parable of the Ship of Shi'ism* (no. 7), and to his classical phase of the *Quintet* (nos. 54, 59, 70), and looks ahead to his later mannerist extremes (nos. 78, 82, 83, 85). He and Shaykh-Muhammad could be described as the psychiatrists among early Safavid artists, so concerned were they with human behavior. A profound portraitist, Mirza-'Ali can be assigned two of the most elegant yet penetrating likenesses in Safavid art, the *Seated Princess with a Spray of Flowers* (no. 70), which is of the same date and spirit as the *Quintet*, and a *Youth with a Golden Pillow* (no. 78), which is the very personification of the Freer Jami, down to the last arch gesture.

It could be argued that early Safavid art struck bottom during the decade between 1564, when Sultan Ibrahim was removed from his governorship of Mashhad, and 1574, when the Shah relented and brought him back as a leading courtier to the capital at Qazvin. For Ibrahim these were years of exile and comparative poverty. But when worldly success fails, art can be sustaining; and his period of trial appears to have been ameliorated by the loyalty of a few of his Mashhad artists, including Shaykh-Muhammad, who continued to paint at his command. Shaykh-Muhammad's *Wayward Youths* (no. 84) probably was drawn for Ibrahim at Sabzavar. This innovatively brilliant sketch, the quintessence of the "evil" mode, is easy to pillory with such loaded epithets as "decadent" or "fin de siècle." In fact, it exemplifies both the end and the beginning of major phases of Safavid art. Its calligraphically sensitive flourishes are at once the last twitches of a dying era and the vulnerable early breaths of another. Their trembling liveliness looks forward to the powerful draftsmanship of Shaykh-Muhammad's artistic heir, Aqa-Riza, later known, after his mighty patron Shah 'Abbas (r. 1587–1629) as Riza 'Abbasi.

Happily, our exhibition ends not with Shaykh-Muhammad's disturbingly ambiguous drawing but with a double-page *Hawking Party* (no. 85) shared between The Metropolitan Museum of Art and the Boston Museum of Fine Arts. It can be dated to a final creative splurge a few years before Shah Tahmasp's death in 1576, when he again became interested in painting. The Shah forgave many of those who had suffered from his puritanical attitudes, and he and Sultan Ibrahim Mirza together encouraged artists. The *Hawking Party* seems to have been the frontispiece to a final great early Safavid manuscript, one now lost. By this festive scene, Mirza-'Ali must have gladdened both uncle and nephew, for it contains elements sufficiently classic for the Shah combined with the intense "baroque" mannerisms encouraged by Sultan Ibrahim.

1. R. H. Pinder-Wilson, *Paintings from the Muslim Courts of India* (London: British Museum, 1976) p. 36, No. 26.

2. For the most complete study of Timurid painting see Ivan V. Stchoukine, *Les Peintures des manuscrits timurides* (Paris: Institut Français d'archeologie de Beyrouth, 1959).

3. *Assault on a Castle*, perhaps by Bihzad. Fogg Art Museum, Bequest—Estate of Abby Aldrich Rockefeller, 1960.199 (31 x 20.2 cm., miniature only).

4. *The Temptation of Wine*, attributable to Bihzad. Fogg Art Museum, Gift—Philip Hofer in honor of Stuart Cary Welch, 1972.299 verso (6.5 x 5 cm., drawing only).

5. Particularly in Albums H. 2153, H. 2160, and H. 2162.

6. Courtesy of the Museum of Fine Arts, Boston. Goloubew Collection, 14.542.

7. Courtesy of the Freer Gallery of Art, Washington, D. C. No. 37.25.

8. Topkapu Sarayi Museum Library. H.762.

9. Three further miniatures from this manuscript are now in the Keir Collection. One is of Turkman date, the others of the Safavid group, of which *The Ascension of the Prophet* is dated the equivalent of 1504/05. These were identified and published by B. W. Robinson. See B. W. Robinson, Ernst J. Grube, G. M. Meredith Owens, R. W. Skelton, and Ivan Stchoukine, *The Keir Collection: Islamic Painting and the Arts of the Book* (London: Faber and Faber, Ltd., 1976).

10. The text and 115 of the original 155 miniatures from this manuscript are in the Museum of Decorative Arts, Tehran (no. 7570). For further information on this important manuscript see Yahyā Zukā, "The Khavarannameh: The Illustrated Copy in the Museum of Decorative Arts." *Hunar-o Mardum* 20 (1343/1964): 17–29. See also Martin Bernard Dickson and Stuart Cary Welch, *The Houghton Shahnama* (Cambridge, Mass.: Harvard University Press, in press), especially Chapter 2 (with notes 7 and 8). The battle scene was formerly on the London art market.

11. This manuscript is in the State Public Library, Leningrad, Dorn 441, Ardabil Collection. For further information see O. F. Akimushkin and A. A. Ivanov, *Persidskie miniatyuri XIV–XVII vv.* (Moscow: Nauka, 1968). See also Dickson and Welch, *The Houghton Shahnama*, especially Chapter 4 (with note 13).

12. See Dickson and Welch, *The Houghton Shahnama*; and Stuart Cary Welch, *A King's Book of Kings: The Shahnameh of Shah Tahmasp* (New York: The Metropolitan Museum of Art, 1972) fig. 14. A diverting caricature of members of the royal household staff, by their employer.

13. Folio 26 verso, after Akimushkin and Ivanov, *Persidskie miniatyuri*, pl. 31.

14. Regrettably, we were unable to borrow Mirza-'Ali's most ambitious and characteristic miniature for the *Book of Kings*, *Nushirvan Receives an Embassy from the King of Hind*, folio 638 recto. For reproductions see Welch, *A King's Book of Kings*, pp. 180–183.

15. No. 46.12. We are grateful to the Freer Gallery of Art, and particularly to its curator of Islamic Art, Dr. Esin Atil, for permission to publish three miniatures from this major manuscript. For a discussion of all the miniatures in this volume, see Dickson and Welch, *The Houghton Shahnama*; for color reproductions, see Stuart Cary Welch, *Persian Painting: Five Royal Safavid Manuscripts of the Sixteenth Century* (New York: Braziller, 1976) pls. 34–48.

16. See Annemarie Schimmel, *Mystical Dimensions of Islam* (Chapel Hill, North Carolina: University of North Carolina Press, 1975) pp. 287–343.

The Catalogue

1. Bound Manuscript: *Dastan-i Jamal u Jalal* by Muhammad 'Asafi

Text completed by the scribe Sultan 'Ali of Qayin at Herat in 1502/03.

110 folios; 34 miniatures (2 dated 1503/04)
Folios measure 270 x 170 mm.
Lent by the University Library of Uppsala (O Nova 2)

Although this manuscript was copied at Herat, which remained the Timurid capital until 1507, its miniatures include the earliest dated Safavid pictures we know that have remained in their manuscript.[1] Only the first picture (*The Sultan in his Divan*, folio 2 verso) lacks the Safavid headgear, although it differs little stylistically from the others except in its calmness of treatment. In all likelihood, the manuscript and its artists changed hands after the completion of the first illustration. History supports this possibility inasmuch as the sons of Sultan-Husayn Bayqara, the last Timurid Sultan, were pitted against him in annual civil wars. One of them, Muhammad-Husayn, cooperated with the Safavids and joined Shah Isma'il in Mazandaran in 1504, at which time he could have brought not only the unfinished manuscript but also its artists to Shah Isma'il. Virtually all of the later pictures, including *Dindar Gives Advice* (folio 5 recto), are charged with Shah Isma'il's visionary fire. This, along with the Safavid headgear, seen here in its earliest stumpy form, attest to the picture's Safavid origin. Already, as can also be seen in a miniature dated within a year of the paintings in this manuscript and added to a Turkman *Khamsa* of Nizami, the Safavid style was vigorously individual, reflecting Shah Isma'il's dynamism and strong direction.[2] We assign the Safavid illustrations of the *Jamal u Jalal* to Sultan-Muhammad and members of his workshop who had already adjusted to their new patron's taste for Turkman vegetation, ornament and extremism. Miniatures such as the *Battle* (folio 26r, fig. 6), however, hark back to the sub-royal idiom known from the late fifteenth-century copy of the *Khavarannama* of Muhammad ibn Husam (fig. 7).

OPPOSITE PAGE: *Dindar Gives Advice*, no. 1, folio 5 recto.

1. Published: K. V. Zetterstéen and C. J. Lamm, *Mohammad 'Asafī: The Story of Jamāl and Jalāl* (Uppsala: Vilhelm Ekmans Universitetsfond, 1948).

2. See Basil W. Robinson, Ernst J. Grube, G. M. Meredith-Owens, R. W. Skelton and Ivan Stchoukine, *The Keir Collection: Islamic Painting and the Arts of the Book* (London: Faber and Faber, Ltd., 1976) no. III, p. 207.

کرسی سیم پر ز نقش و نگار
وزرا پیش خسرو ایام
قفل از درج معرفت بگشای
هان چه داری بیا و پیش بیار
خواست بر پا فراز کرسی سیم
گفت این پند و نطق کرد آواز
پاسبانت هلال و دربان بدر
دولتت را بدهر لطف آله
ادهم طبع را دهم جولان
پند گویم بمنطق موزون
بلطافت چو لؤلؤ مکنون

بنهادند خاصهٔ دیندار
گفت پس باز با دیندار
بسخن نقد خویشتن بنمای
با وزیر این سخن چو سلطان گفت
کرد آغاز پند مرد حکیم

پند دادن پندار جلال را

طلعت ماه و چون سپهر سریر
دارد از چشم زخم چرخ نگاه
گوی معنی بصولجان سخن

شاه چون بر سریر کرد آرام
که دُر نطق کن ببزم نثار
گوهر معنوی بکن ایثار
خاک راهش بنوک مژگان رفت
کرد صندوق گوهرش سرباز
ای شه مهر رای گردون قدر
مطربت زهره است و مادح تیر
گر اشارت بود ز شاه جهان
بربایم ز فاضلان بسخن

2. Rustam Sleeping While Rakhsh Fights the Lion

From a BOOK OF KINGS apparently commissioned by Shah Isma'il
Attributable to Sultan-Muhammad

Ca. 1515–22
318 x 208 mm.
By courtesy of the Trustees of the British Museum (1948.12.11.023)

The rash young Shah, Kay Ka'us, initiated a mission to destroy the divs of Mazandaran which resulted in his being taken captive. To rescue him Rustam set out on the shorter but more dangerous route to Mazandaran. The hero pressed forward until fatigue overtook him and then lay down to sleep in a pasture. Unknowingly, Rustam had chosen the lair of a ferocious lion as his temorary bed. While he slept, the lion returned and attacked Rakhsh, who dug his teeth into the lion's back and trampled him to death. Awakened by the commotion, Rustam chided Rakhsh for so risking his life after which the two returned to their naps. S. R. C.

This thrilling miniature exemplifies Shah Isma'il's visionary taste during the later years of his reign, when Prince Tahmasp served as nominal governor of Herat. Vivid in coloring, expressive rather than naturalistic in the drawing of Rustam, the horse, and the lion, and alive with hidden animal-spirits peeping from rocks and tree trunks, its style emerged naturally from the *Jamal u Jalal* pictures. By now, however, the impact of Shah Isma'il's patronage and of the Turkman metropolitan tradition is even more apparent.

Intriguingly, Sultan-Muhammad's earlier pictures for Shah Tahmasp's *Book of Kings* (see nos. 9 and 10) are strikingly similar in style to the *Sleeping Rustam*. Indeed, *Hushang Slays the Black Div* (no. 9), with all its indebtednesses to the *Khavarannama* and *Jamal u Jalal*, might well be from the same manuscript. It seems likely, therefore, that the *Sleeping Rustam* and its unfinished companion pictures[1] were intended for a great manuscript in preparation for Shah Isma'il—a manuscript that he later gave to, or shared with, Tahmasp, on the prince's return from Herat in 1522, and which later gained renown as the great *Shahnama* of Shah Tahmasp.

1. See Philipp Walter Schulz, *Die persisch-islamische Miniaturmalerei: ein Beitrag zur Kunstgeschichte Irans* (Leipzig: Karl W. Hiersemann, 1914) Vol. II, pls. 47, 48, 49. These pictures are consistent in size with those of the Houghton manuscript.

سوی رخش رخشان بیامد دمان
چو آتش بجوشید رخش آن زمان
دو دست اندر آورد و زد بر سرش
همان تیز دندان به پشت اندرش
همی زدش بر خاک تا پاره کرد
ددی را بدان چاره بیچاره کرد
چو بیدار شد رستم تیز چنگ
جهان دید بر شیر تاریک و تنگ
چنین گفت کای رخش ناهوشیار
که گفتت که با شیر کن کارزار
اگر تو شدی کشته در دست اوی
من این ببر و این مغفر جنگجوی
چگونه کشیدی به مازندران
کمند کیانی و گرز گران
سرم گر ز خواب خوش آگه شدی
ترا جنگ با شیر کوته شدی
چو خورشید برزد سر از تیره کوه
تهمتن ز خواب خوش آمد ستوه
تن رخش بستر دو زین برنهاد
ز یزدان نیکی دهش کرد یاد
یکی راه پیش آمدش ناگزیر
همی رفت باید بر خیره خیر

The Houghton Shahnama

The *Shahnama* ("Book of Kings"), the Iranian national epic, was begun by Daqiqi, who composed a few thousand lines before his untimely death, and completed by Abu'l Qasim Firdawsi of Tus in over 50,000 rhyming couplets in 1010 A.D. This copy, known as "The Houghton *Shahnama*," belonged to Shah Tahmasp, whose titles appear in several places, including the opening rosette (folio 16 recto, no. 5). Although the manuscript contains no colophon, one of the miniatures (folio 516 verso, no. 30) is dated 934 A.H./1527/28 A.D., but the project seems to have been in progress from c. 1522, or earlier, until c. 1535, after which two of its two hundred and fifty-eight miniatures were added (between 1535 and 1540, see nos. 27 and 31). No scribe's name is given and only two of the miniatures are signed: folio 60 verso by Mir Musavvir, and folio 521 verso by Dust-Muhammad (no. 31). The others can be attributed on stylistic grounds to the Tabriz court artists: Sultan-Muhammad, Mir Musavvir, Aqa-Mirak, Dust-Muhammad, Mirza-'Ali, Muzaffar-'Ali, Shaykh-Muhammad, Mir Sayyid-'Ali, 'Abd us-Samad, Qadimi, Qasim son of 'Ali (?), 'Abd ul-Vahhab, 'Abd ul-'Aziz (?), Bashdan Qara (?) and Mirza Muhammad (?). When complete, the manuscript contained 380 folios, each measuring about 470 by 318 mm.: text areas, inside marginal rulings, average 269 by 170 mm.. (Measurements given for individual miniatures are taken at maximum points of the painted surface.)

This manuscript was presented by Shah Tahmasp in 1568 to Sultan Selim II, and it remained in the Ottoman Library at least until 1801, when Mehmed 'Arif, "Keeper of the Guns" at the Palace Treasury, finished writing synopses of the subjects on the protective pages of the miniatures. By 1903, it was in the collection of Baron Edmond de Rothschild, one of whose descendants sold it in 1959 to Arthur A. Houghton, Jr.. Mr. Houghton subsequently presented 78 of its miniatures to the Metropolitan Museum of Art. Others now belong to the Museum for Islamic Art, Dahlem, and to several private collectors.[1]

OPPOSITE PAGE: Detail of *Court of the Gayumars* (no. 8).

1. To be published: Martin Bernard Dickson and Stuart Cary Welch, *The Houghton Shahnameh* (Cambridge, Mass.: Harvard University Press, in press).

3. Double Page Frontispiece to the Baysunghur Introduction

From Shah Tahmasp's BOOK OF KINGS, folios 2 verso and 3 recto

Ca. 1530–35
470 x 318 mm. (each folio)
Lent by Arthur A. Houghton, Jr.

Like a sumptuous and majestic carpet stretched out to welcome those fortunate enough to view this royal manuscript, the double page *'unwan* represents the sustained efforts of at least two important but anonymous masters: the calligrapher, who may have been Mahmud of Nishapur, who later copied the British Library *Quintet* (nos. 48–65), and the illuminator. In Iran, fine writing, in this case in *nasta'liq* script, was at least as much admired as painting; and the masters of illumination, whose floral arabesques, richly colored margins, and elegantly proportioned fields of lapis lazuli here set the austerely splendid mood for one of Iran's noblest manuscripts, were also revered. The Introduction to this as well as many other copies of the *Shahnama* was composed in the early fifteenth century for Prince Baysunghur, another major Persianate[1] bibliophile.[2]

OPPOSITE PAGE: no. 3, folio 2 verso.

1. For use of the term "Persianate," see Marshal Hodgson, *The Venture of Islam: Conscience and History in a World Civilization*, 3 vols. (Chicago: University of Chicago Press, 1972)

2. His superb and lavishly illustrated copy of the *Book of Kings* is in the Imperial Library of Iran. A facsimile edition was published in connection with the celebration of the 2500th anniversary of the founding of the Persian Empire by Cyrus the Great. See: *The Shahnameh of Ferdowsi, The Baysongheri Manuscript: An Album of Miniatures and Illuminations, Completed in 833 A.H./A.D. 1430 and Preserved in the Imperial Library, Tehrān* (Tehran, 1971).

افتتاح سخن آن به که کنند اهل کمال
به ثنای ملک الملک خدای متعال
مالک الملکی که در تدبیر ملک و ملکوت و ترتیب عالم لاهوت
و ناسوت بوزیر و مشیر و ظهیر و نصیر محتاج و مفتقر نگشت
پادشاهی و سلطنت او را مسلم است که ملک سرمد او از تنقیص
زوال و نکبت و تحویل و انتقال مصون و مامون است حشمت
و عظمتش از مذلت انقضا و مهانت انقطاع و انتها معرا و مبرا
پادشاهی که پادشاهان را
پادشاهی ز فیض نعمت اوست

4. *Firdawsi Encounters the Court Poets of Ghazna*

From Shah Tahmasp's BOOK OF KINGS, folio 7 recto
Attributable to Aqa-Mirak

Ca. 1532
267 x 232 mm. (miniature only)
Private Collection

Seeking patronage for the completion of his Book of Kings, *Firdawsi went to Ghazna, the capital of Sultan Mahmud, who—by happy coincidence—wished to employ the most talented poet of the era to compose an epic on the pre-Muslim kings of Iran. Upon his arrival, Firdawsi chanced upon three of Sultan Mahmud's court poets picnicking in a garden. Considering him a boorish outsider, and, when they learned he was a poet, a possible rival besides, they challenged him to add the last line to an extremely difficult quatrain. His solution was so brilliant that they reluctantly accepted him. In due course, Firdawsi also impressed the Sultan, who granted him the commission.* S. R. C.

According to Dust-Muhammad, Aqa-Mirak was among those "privileged to approach" the person of the Shah. Furthermore, "At the House of Painting he but picks up his brush and depicts for us pictures of unparalleled delight. . . . Good Lord! The Glory of this painter! What God-given Might!" Considering this lavish praise from a fellow artist who was also one of the inner circle, it is not surprising that Aqa-Mirak was honored by being assigned the task of painting the first picture in the Shah's *Book of Kings, Firdawsi Encounters the Court Poets of Ghazna.*[1] Apparently he reciprocated by including a portrait of the Shah himself, the elegant young man surveying the scene at the far right, as the first figure among the thousands who appear in the royal manuscript. The style of the picture and the age of the young man, if we are correct in the identification, point to about the year 1532, when Shah Tahmasp was eighteen and still beardless. The same royal countenance, somewhat older, was painted by Aqa-Mirak as Khusraw in the Shah's *Quintet* (nos. 56 and 58).

OPPOSITE PAGE: Detail of no. 4. Illustration of the complete miniature, frontispiece.

1. For color plates of this miniature and 16 others from Shah Tahmasp's *Book of Kings*, see Dickson and Welch, *The Houghton Shahnameh*. Also see Stuart Cary Welch, *A King's Book of Kings: The Shahnameh of Shah Tahmasp* (New York: The Metropolitan Museum of Art, 1972) pp. 80, 83.

برسم
كتابخانه السلطان الاعظم
والخاقان الاعدل الاكرم
السلطان بن السلطان بن السلطان ابو
المظفر السلطان شاه طهماسب الحسيني
الصفوي بهادر خان خلد
الله تعالى ملكه وسلطانه

5. Rosette

From Shah Tahmasp's BOOK OF KINGS, folio 16 recto

Ca. 1535
470 x 318 mm.
Lent by Arthur A. Houghton, Jr.

This sunburst of ornament, probably by the same illuminator as the double-page frontispiece, is inscribed in white *nasta'liq* with very much the same formulaic titles found on a miniature in Shah Tahmasp's *Quintet* (see no. 57, folio 60 verso). It was placed following the Baysunghur Introduction, but before Firdawsi's opening verses (which are also sumptuously illuminated), on the verso side of the same folio (no. 6).[1]

Inscribed

upper cartouche

In His Name, the Most Praised and Most Exalted!

within rosette

Commissioned for the Library of the most mighty Sultan, and the most beneficent [Grand Khan], Khaqan, Sultan, son and grandson of sultans, [The Victorious], Abu'l-Muzaffar, Sultan Shah Tahmasp, of Husayni and Safavi descent [The Valiant] Bahadur Khan. May God the Most Exalted, perpetuate his realm and his rule, and diffuse. . . .

lower cartouche

. . . . his justice and his benevolence throughout the world!

1. For a color reproduction, see Welch, *A King's Book of Kings*, p. 78.

6. Opening Verses: *In Praise of God and the Intellect*

From Shah Tahmasp's BOOK OF KINGS, folio 16 verso

Ca. 1535
470 x 318 mm.
Lent by Arthur A. Houghton, Jr.

The *Shahnama* opens thus: *In the name of the Lord-creator of the Soul and the Intellect* and is followed by a eulogy of the Universal Intelligence and the Universal Soul. These noble lines were enriched by the most inventive illumination in the volume, a sunrise of arabesque with flowering tendrils and cloud bands mounted over a stunning panel of similar motifs enlivened with animal masks and grotesques. This configuration is supported by three intercolumnar bands, such as are occasionally found on other pages of the manuscript.

Inscribed

in upper cartouche
The Beginning of the Book, the Shahnama

in lower cartouche
Chapter in Praise of the Intellect

آغاز کتاب شاهنامه

بنام خداوند جان و خرد ‌ ‌ کزین برتر اندیشه برنگذرد

خداوند کیهان و گردان سپهر ‌ ‌ فروزنده ماه و ناهید و مهر

خداوند نام و خداوند جای ‌ ‌ خداوند روزی ده رهنمای

ز نام و نشان و گمان برترست ‌ ‌ نگارنده بر شده گوهرست

به بینندگان آفریننده را ‌ ‌ نه بینی مرنجان دو بیننده را

نیابد بدو نیز اندیشه راه ‌ ‌ که او برتر از نام و از جایگاه

سخن هر چه زین گوهران بگذرد ‌ ‌ نیابد بدو راه جان و خرد

خرد گر سخن برگزیند همی ‌ ‌ همان را ستاید که بیند همی

ستودن نیارد کس او را چو هست ‌ ‌ میان بندگی را ببایدت بست

خرد را و جان را همی سنجد او ‌ ‌ در اندیشه سخته کی گنجد او

بدین آلت و رای و جان و زبان ‌ ‌ ستود آفریننده را چون توان

بهستیش باید که خستو شوی ‌ ‌ ز گفتار و پیکار یکسو شوی

چو پوینده باشی و جوینده راه ‌ ‌ بفرمانها ژرف کردن نگاه

توانا بود هر که دانا بود ‌ ‌ ز دانش دل پیر برنا بود

ازین پرده برتر سخن گاه نیست ‌ ‌ ز هستی مر اندیشه را راه نیست

کنون ای خردمند وصف خرد ‌ ‌ بدین جایگه گفتن اندر خورد

کنون تا چه داری بیار از خرد ‌ ‌ که گوش نیوشنده زو برخورد

خرد بهتر از هر چه ایزدت داد ‌ ‌ ستایش خرد را به از راه داد

خرد افسر شهریاران بود ‌ ‌ خرد زیور نامداران بود

خرد رهنمای و خرد دلگشای ‌ ‌ خرد دست گیرد بهر دو سرای

ازو شادمانی وزو مردمیست ‌ ‌ ازویت فزونی وزویت کمیست

خرد تیره و مرد روشن روان ‌ ‌ نباشد همی شادمان یک زمان

چه گفت آن خردمند مرد خرد ‌ ‌ که دانا ز گفتار او برخورد

کسی کو خرد را ندارد ز پیش ‌ ‌ دلش گردد از کرده خویش ریش

هشیوار دیوانه خواند ورا ‌ ‌ همان خویش بیگانه داند ورا

ازویی بهر دو سرای ارجمند ‌ ‌ گسسته خرد پای دارد به بند

7. Parable of the Ship of Shi'ism

From Shah Tahmasp's BOOK OF KINGS, folio 18 verso
Attributable to Mirza-'Ali

Ca. 1530
300 x 209 mm. (miniature only)
Lent by The Metropolitan Museum of Art, Gift of Arthur A. Houghton, Jr., 1970 (1970.301.1)

Firdawsi's Shahnama *opens with praise of God in both philosophical and theological terms. In the theological section Firdawsi relates a parable about the passengers on seventy ships wrecked in a stormy sea from which no one emerged alive. Each of the ships held believers in one of the seventy religions of man. The finest and largest of all the ships carried Muhammad, 'Ali, Hasan, and Husayn; and this was the ship on which Firdawsi chose to travel. Although the ship and its passengers were doomed to destruction, Firdawsi rode content in the knowledge that he would perish near the helping hands of his saviours.* S. R. C.

Although the work of illustrating the *Shahnama* ordinarily proceeded chronologically, from the beginning of the epic to the end, particularly admired pictures were inserted later, at the patron's discretion. This miniature, the third in the volume, can be attributed on grounds of style to Mirza-'Ali, a brilliant painter of the second Safavid generation, who was over-shadowed by his great father, Sultan-Muhammad. Contemporary sources tend to remark upon his parentage, then dismiss him with modest praise. Nonetheless, his art was favored by the Shah and later by the Shah's nephew, the great patron Sultan Ibrahim Mirza. Mirza-'Ali's earlier works for the *Shahnama* must have been painted when he was very young. This one may well mark his artistic coming-of-age, and is one of his more ambitious compositions for the manuscript.[1] Although influenced by his father's style, Mirza-'Ali here reveals the impact of Shaykh-Zadeh (see no. 42), a pupil of Bihzad whose version of that master's style was strongly felt by the second generation of Safavid artists.[2]

Inscribed

along the canopy on top deck of main ship, rhyming couplet from Sa'di's Preface to his *Rose Garden*

> *What need are walls?*
> *Muhammad's here to fortify our inner state!*
> *Why heed the waves when Noah's fore, piloting our Ship of State?*

on lintel of gateway leading to upper deck

> *May the portals of this court ever open to good fortune!*

1. For color reproductions, see Welch, *A King's Book of Kings*, pp. 85, 86.

2. For an apt comparison to this picture, see *Iskandar Shooting a Bird from a Boat*, a picture attributable to Shaykh-Zadeh in the Paris *Collected Works* of Nava'i (Bibliothèque Nationale, supp. turc, 316, 317); also, see Stuart Cary Welch, *Persian Painting: Five Royal Safavid Manuscripts of the Sixteenth Century* (New York: Braziller, 1976) fig. B.

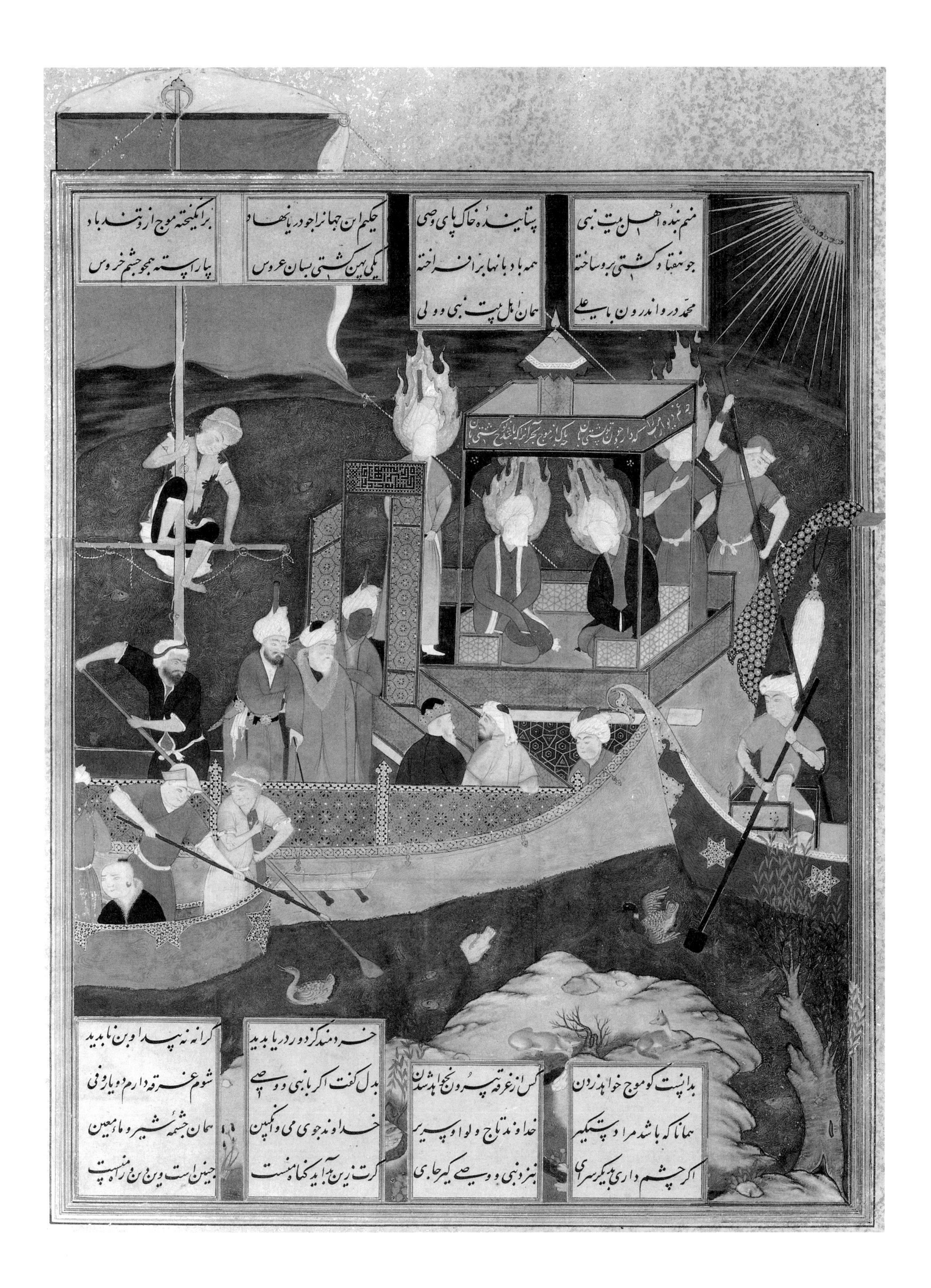
منم بندهٔ اهل بیت نبی
پستایندهٔ خاک پای وصی
حکیم این جهان را چو دریا نهاد
برانگیخته موج ازو تند باد
چو هفتاد کشتی برو ساخته
همه بادبانها برافراخته
یکی پهن کشتی بسان عروس
بیاراسته همچو چشم خروس
محمد درو اندرون با علی
همان اهل بیت نبی و ولی
خردمند کز دور دریا بدید
کرانه نه پیدا و بن ناپدید
بدانست کو موج خواهد زدن
کس از غرقه بیرون نخواهد شدن
بدل گفت اگر با نبی و وصی
شوم غرقه دارم دو یار وفی
همانا که باشد مرا دستگیر
خداوند تاج و لوا و سریر
خداوند جوی می و انگبین
همان چشمهٔ شیر و ماء معین
اگر چشم داری بدیگر سرای
بنزد نبی و وصی گیر جای
گرت زین بد آید گناه منست
چنین است و این دین و راه منست

8. *The Court of Gayumars*

From Shah Tahmasp's BOOK OF KINGS, folio 20 verso
By Sultan-Muhammad

Ca. 1522–25
342 x 231 mm. (miniature only)
Lent by Arthur A. Houghton, Jr.

Gayumars, the first Shah of Iran, ruled the world from a mountain top for thirty years. During his benevolent reign, men wore leopard skin garments and discovered how to prepare food. Gayumars' subjects revered him and in his presence wild animals grew meek as lambs. In time, however, a plot by the evil demon Ahriman shattered the idyllic peace. Although the angel Surush tried to warn the Shah of Ahriman's schemes, the ferocious Black Div, son of Ahriman, killed Siyamak, Gayumars' beloved son. S. R. C.

In this astonishing picture, Sultan-Muhammad brought together the visionary power of Turkman painting, so admired by Shah Isma'il, and the psychological nuances and fineness associated with Bihzad, whose style was favored by Prince Tahmasp. In it, the Western and Eastern traditions of Iranian painting merged; and Safavid painting reached its greatest height. In his Preface to the Bahram Mirza Album, Dust-Muhammad's appreciation of Sultan-Muhammad could hardly be more laudatory. With him "painting rises to the heights, where skies, for all their thousand-starred eyes, have yet to see the like. . . . Among his creative works are those he painted and sketched in a *Shahnama* done for his Alexandrous Majesty in whose person is Jamshid's right reserved, the True Creed conserved, and the True Rite preserved." One of these (*Gayumars*), described as "a scene with figures clad in leopard skins," is singled out for special praise: "Lions fierce in the field of painting, as awesome tigers drawn to the arts, stung at heart by the smart of his brush, cower in hurt, overpowered by this work."

To see the picture is to agree with Dust-Muhammad. Each rocky outcropping, flamelike tree, figure, and blossom proclaims the artist's wizardry, and rewards our sustained contemplation. All ages and sorts of men peep out at us, as do hundreds of chthonic spirits concealed in rocks, in what must be the most profound and yet delightful game of hide and seek ever devised.[1]

OPPOSITE PAGE: Detail of no. 8. Illustration of the complete miniature, p. 17.

1. For color reproductions, see Welch, *A King's Book of Kings*, pp. 89, 91.

9. *Hushang Slays the Black Div*

From Shah Tahmasp's BOOK OF KINGS, folio 21 verso
Attributable to Sultan-Muhammad

Ca. 1522 or earlier
321 x 215 mm. (miniature only)
Private Collection

Snarls, quacks, yelps, growls, thuds, and trumpeting sound the death of the Black Div, wolf-like son of Ahriman, who is shown being decapitated by Hushang, in partial vengeance against the Div's master, Ahriman (see no. 8). To the right, Gayumars, still lamenting his son's death, proudly observes his grandson's valor. Lions, leopards, bears, wolves, and angels assist; and the sky vibrates with the flapping of cranes, ducks, and other excited birds (see color detail, p. 6). Even the grotesques in the rocks chorus their approval.[1]

Dashingly sketched and spontaneously conceived, this miniature is the liveliest of a series painted by Sultan-Muhammad for the *Shahnama*, paradigms of energy, intended either to charm the boy-patron Tahmasp, or to excite his visionary father, Shah Isma'il. In style, these exhilarating pictures recall *Rustam Sleeping While Rakhsh Fights the Lion* (no. 2), which probably was begun for the same project. Although the doll-like simplifications of figures recall the *Khavarannama* (see fig. 7) and *Jamal u Jalal* (no. 1, fig. 6), Sultan-Muhammad's sharp-eyed observation of nature is apparent in the gestures of the cranes and in the musculature of a white demon's back.

1. For color reproduction, see Stuart Cary Welch *Persian Painting: Five Royal Safavid Manuscripts of the Sixteenth Century* (New York: Braziller, 1976) pl. 4.

سیامک خجسته یکی پور داشت ٭ که نزد نیا جای دستور داشت

گرانمایه را نام هوشنگ بود ٭ تو گفتی همه هوش و فرهنگ بود

نیا پروریده مر او را به بر ٭ بنزد نیا یادگار پدر

نیایش بجای پسر داشتی ٭ جز او بر کسی چشم نگماشتی

چو بنهاد دل کینه و جنگ را ٭ بخواند آن گرانمایه هوشنگ را

همه گفتنیها بدو باز گفت ٭ همه رازها برگشاد از نهفت

که من لشکری کرد خواهم همی ٭ خروشی برآورد خواهم همی

ترا بود باید همی پیشرو ٭ که من رفتنی‌ام تو سالار نو

جنگ هوشنگ با دیو

پری و پلنگ انجمن کرد و شیر ٭ ز درندگان نیز گرگ دلیر

سپهبد ابر کین و کند آوری ٭ سپاهی دد و دام و مرغ و پری

پس پشت لشکر کیومرث شاه ٭ نبیره به پیش اندرون با سپاه

بیامد سیه دیو با ترس و باک ٭ همی به آسمان برپراکند خاک

ز هرای درندگان جنگ دیو ٭ شده سست و از خشم کیهان خدیو

10. *The Death of King Mardas*

From Shah Tahmasp's BOOK OF KINGS, folio 25 verso
Attributable to Sultan-Muhammad

Ca. 1522 or earlier
232 x 175 mm. (miniature only)
Lent by Arthur A. Houghton, Jr.

The moods of the *Shahnama* range from heroism, joy, and wisdom to lust, cruelty, and wickedness. *The Death of King Mardas* is of the last sort—here interpreted with humor and bitter-sweetness by Sultan-Muhammad. Iblis (Satan), disguised as the old gentleman to the left, persuaded Prince Zuhhak, gazing down from the balcony, to join in a plot against his father, Mardas, a king of Arabia Deserta, in order to inherit the throne. A deep pit was dug, carefully screened with boughs, in the pathway used every day at dawn by the old king en route to his bath. The plot succeeded; Mardas fell to his death, to the consternation of his pageboy, who peers somewhat vapidly into the pit, candle in hand.

This is another of Sultan-Muhammad's spritely early miniatures for the *Shahnama*. In it he has sketched a witch-dance of foliage setting the mood for a dastardly act. A gloriously seething cluster of flowers and leaves, to the right of Iblis's head, is one of the artist's liveliest recollections of a favorite Turkman motif (see color detail). His sure, calligraphic sweep of line appears to advantage in the festooning robes of the ill-fated Mardas.

OPPOSITE PAGE: Detail of no. 10.
Complete miniature at right.

11. *The Nightmare of Zuhhak*

From Shah Tahmasp's BOOK OF KINGS, folio 28 verso
Attributable to Mir Musavvir

Ca. 1525–35
342 x 276 mm. (miniature only)
Private Collection

Gullible Zuhhak gained his father's throne—at a price. Iblis, having plotted the murder, later turned up as a chef and prepared succulent dishes for the royal gastronome. So pleased was Zuhhak that he offered the cook any boon he desired. The chef wished merely to kiss his patron's shoulders, but when he did, two snakes, who required daily feedings of the brains of human youths, grew where the devil's lips had touched.

One night, gray with age and torment, Zuhhak awoke in terror from a nightmare. In his dream, he had been beaten with an ox-head mace, yoked, and dragged through the dust past jeering crowds to Mount Damavand. S. R. C.

Dust-Muhammad in his *Preface* to the Bahram Mirza Album describes Mir Musavvir as a "master jeweler . . . a star of lapis lazuli . . . a Sayyid [descendant of the Prophet] whose brushwork is flawless . . . ," clearly the artistic personality represented here. Mir Musavvir's *Nightmare* is a tour de force, a painted challenge to Sultan-Muhammad's *The Court of the Gayumars* (no. 8). Despite the subject, it is the high point of Mir Musavvir's romanticism; he has concentrated on the king's pleasure dome, which may be an idealized view of Shah Tahmasp's court and is perhaps the most ambitious treatment of architecture in Safavid painting. The artist has rendered night by the crescent moon and by a deeply saturated, nocturnal palette. Signs of doom are minimal, but if we follow Zuhhak's gaze to the patch of garden, lower right, each stone reveals a microcosm of ghouls.[1]

1. For color reproductions, see Welch, *A King's Book of Kings*, pp. 101, 103.

بجستند خورشید رویان ز جای
ازان نامور نعرهٔ کدخدای
چنین گفت ضحاک را ارنواز
که شاها چه بودت نکویی براز

12. *Faridun Crosses the River Dijla*

From Shah Tahmasp's BOOK OF KINGS, folio 33 verso
Attributable to Sultan-Muhammad

Ca. 1525–30
271 x 207 mm.
Private Collection

Zuhhak's nightmare was interpreted by his leading magus as a prophecy that a champion named Faridun would seize the throne. Despite Zuhhak's efforts to locate and slay the still youthful rebel, Faridun grew up unscathed; and at sixteen he undertook the revolt against Zuhhak. While his great army gathered, Faridun procured an ox-headed mace, and soon led his troops toward Arabia. At the bank of the River Dijla (Tigris) the Arab boatmen who controlled the ferries refused passage to Faridun and his army for Zuhhak's orders specified that only those authorized by him might cross. Undaunted, Faridun and his horse pressed onward into the river, followed by his reluctant supporters.

S. R. C.

Sultan-Muhammad's easy adjustment to the Herat style of Bihzad, admired by Shah Tahmasp, is apparent in this complex, strikingly designed miniature. The expressively distorted, lumpy figures of his earlier mode (see nos. 2, 8, 9, 41, 43, 44) have now become slenderly naturalistic. Three-dimensional space has taken on a modicum of Bihzad's coherence and logic; and the finish is jewel-like rather than boldly dashing. Nevertheless, close scrutiny shows that the changes were superficial. The free-flowing line of the boatman's clothing is but a finer version of Mardas's (no. 10); and Sultan-Muhammad's sense of the comical, which had been toned down in his transitional pictures,[1] has re-emerged in scarcely subtler form. An amusing young horseman, center right, gestures insolently towards a corpulent veteran who is terrified of entering the water.

In the foreground, a pair of lions—stylistic ancestors of the seventeenth- and eighteenth-century beasts from the Indian school of Kotah—stalk through ornamental grasses, silhouetted against the now tarnished silver river. Close inspection brings out many waterbirds and leaping fish, the latter made to appear glisteningly wet with crushed mother-of-pearl or mica. An almost invisible, ghostly monkey bobs playfully on a flowering branch to the right of the central standard, and the concealed grotesques in the stony horizon recall those of *The Court of Gayumars.*

1. Compare: Welch, *A King's Book of Kings,* pp. 104–111.

که کشتی و زورق هم اندر شتاب / گذارند یکسر برین روی آب
بدان تازیان گفت پیروزشاه / که کشتی درافکن هم اکنون براه

مرا با سپاهم بدانسو رسان / از اینها کسی را بدین سو ممان
نیاورد کشتی نگهبان رود / نیامد بگفت فریدون فرود

چنان یافت پاسخ که شاه جهان / چنین گفت با من سخن در نهان
مرا گفت کشتی مران تا نخست / جوازی بیابی بمهر درست

فریدون چو بشنید شد خشمناک / از آن ژرف دریا نیامدش باک
بتندی میان کیانی ببست / بر آن تازی شیر دل برنشست

سرش تیز شد کینه و جنگ را / به آب اندر افگند گلرنگ را
ببستند یارانش یکسر کمر / همیدون بدریا نهادند سر

بر آن بادپایان با آفرین / به آب اندرون غرقه کردند زین
سر سرکشان اندر آمد بخواب / ز ناهیدن چارپایان آب

به آب اندرون آورد و یال / چنان چون شب تیره بازی خیال
بخشکی رسیدند سر کینه جوی / به بیت المقدس نهادند روی

13. *The Death of Zuhhak*

From Shah Tahmasp's BOOK OF KINGS, folio 37 verso
Attributable to Sultan-Muhammad, assisted by Mir Sayyid-'Ali

Ca. 1535
311 x 232 mm. (miniature only)
Private Collection

When Faridun's army took Zuhhak's palace, Zuhhak had fled, but Faridun still followed the victory with feasts and entertained Zuhhak's favorite ladies, the daughters of Jamshid. Tortured by jealousy, Zuhhak disguised himself and stole into the palace to murder the daughters. On advice from archangel Surush, Faridun spared Zuhhak, bound him in chains, and carried him to Mount Damavand. Zuhhak was fastened, arms outstretched, in a remote cave, "so that his brain might chafe and his agony endure" forever. S. R. C.

Like Shakespeare, Sultan-Muhammad populated his dramas with a large and varied cast. Although on the whole very life-like, some of his characters veer from conventional interpretations. Here Zuhhak the Dragon-king seems to accept his agony unflinchingly, while Faridun raises an admonishing finger. As in Mir Musavvir's *Nightmare* (no. 11), ambience belies action. Despite the dragonish clouds, the weather is bright and cheery and the elegant hawking party seems better suited to a picnic than to a death scene. But there is horror too in the stealthy, cruel-mouthed executioners and, as in *Gayumars* (no. 8), the mountain crags surprise us with their earth-spirits.

This haunting miniature is probably the latest major contribution to the manuscript by Sultan-Muhammad. In style, it could as well belong to the British Library *Quintet* of 1539 to 1543 (nos. 48, 65). Mir Sayyid-'Ali, an aspiring young painter recognized for his painstaking workmanship, evidently help finish the work. Many of the faces, trees, and ornamental passages are his.[1]

Detail of no. 13.

1. For color reproductions, see Welch, *A King's Book of Kings*, pp. 117, 119; and Welch, *Persian Painting*, pl. 6.

فروبست دستش بآن کوه باز
بدان تا بماند بسختی دراز
بماند او برین گونه آویخته
وزو خون دل بر زمین ریخته
بیا تا جهان را ببد نسپریم
بکوشش همه دست نیکی بریم
نباشد همی نیک و بد پایدار
همان به که نیکی بود یادگار
سخن ماند از تو همی یادگار
سخن را چنین خوارمایه مدار

14. *Faridun in the Guise of a Dragon Tests His Sons*

From Shah Tahmasp's BOOK OF KINGS, folio 42 verso
Attributable to Aqa-Mirak

Ca. 1535
292 x 283 mm. (miniature only)
Private Collection

The daughters of Jamshid bore Faridun three sons who grew to be tall as cypresses and noble in demeanor. When they reached marriageable age, they were sent to the Yemen to marry three royal sisters of unmatched beauty. While returning to Iran with their brides, the three princes were accosted by a fire-breathing dragon—Faridun in disguise, testing their mettle.

When Faridun turned on his first son, the young man fled in terror, exclaiming that no one in his right mind would fight a dragon. The second son drew his sword and shouted that it made no difference whether he did battle with a raging lion or a cavalier. The third son faced the dragon and proclaimed, "Be off! You are a mere crocodile; beware of lions! If you have ever heard of Faridun, you will not dare fight us. For we are his sons, and each of us is a warrior like him!"

From this test Faridun gleaned the true character of each of his sons, and he named each one accordingly: the one who sought safety, Salm; the youth who displayed brazen fearlessness, Tur; and the moderate son who kept his wits about him, Iraj. Each of the three received one third of Faridun's kingdom: to Tur went the eastern portion, Turan; to Salm, the western provinces, Rum; and to Iraj, the central kingdom, Iran. S. R. C.

Of all the Shah's artists, Aqa-Mirak was said to have been closest to him. His full name—Aqa-Jamal ud-Din-Mirak the Husayni (or Hasani) the Isfahani—proclaims that he belonged to an Isfahan family descended from the Prophet's grandson. Dust-Muhammad, in his famed Preface of 1544/45, commented upon this painter's portraiture: "As for his likenesses—and where are their like?—as the farseeing view them, they are foremost in sight." This talent invites speculation as to the identities of the personages portrayed here; for each of Faridun's sons is true to life. Two of them, the lightly mustachioed and the black-bearded, recur frequently in Aqa-Mirak's pictures, which suggests that they were well-known to him. Another of his favorite motifs is the toothily gloating smile of dragonish Faridun, that reappears on the face of the triumphant physician in the *Quintet* (no. 53) and again on a pleased hare befriended by Majnun (no. 62).

His latest and most lovingly finished miniature for the *Shahnama*, this picture was Aqa-Mirak's reply to Sultan-Muhammad's *Gayumars*. For it, he created some of the most splendid animals in Iranian art: a mighty but benevolent dragon; three supremely elegant horses; a humorously outraged bear; a noble ibex; and a timid, scared rabbit. Set against a golden, dusky sky the inhabited cliffs and rocks vie with Sultan-Muhammad's psychologically absorbing fantasies.[1]

1. For color reproductions, see Welch, *A King's Book of Kings*, pp. 121, 122.

خروشان و جوشان بجوش درون / همی از دهانش آمد آتش برون
چو هر سه پسر را بنزدیک دید / بگرد اندرون کوه تاریک دید
برانگیخت گرد و برآورد جوش / جهان گشت از آوای او پرخروش
بیامد دمان سوی مهتر پسر / که او بود پرمایه و تاجور
پسر گفت با اژدها روز جنگ / نپارد خردیافته مرد سنگ
سبک پشت بنمود و بگریخت زو / پدر زی برادرش بنهاد روی
میانه برادر چو او را بدید / سبک تیغ تیز از میان برکشید
بدل گفت اگر کارزارست کار / چه شیر دمنده چه جنگی سوار
همی خواست با او نبرد آورد / پر اژدها را بگرد آورد
چو کهتر پسر نزد ایشان رسید / خروشید کان اژدها را بدید
بدو گفت کز پیش ما دور شو / نهنگی تو بر راه شیران مرو
گرت نام شاه آفریدون بگوش / رسیدست با ما بدینسان مکوش
که فرزند اوییم هر سه پسر / همه گرزداران پرخاشخر
گر از راه بیراه یکسو شوی / رهد جانت از نیزهٔ چنبری
فریدون فرخ چو بشنید و دید / هنرها بدانست شد ناپدید

15. *Tur Beheads Iraj*

From Shah Tahmasp's BOOK OF KINGS, folio 48 verso
Attributable to Sultan-Muhammad

Ca. 1530–35
330 x 233 mm. (miniature only)
Lent by Arthur A. Houghton, Jr.

As the years passed, Salm and Tur grew envious of the attention Faridun paid Iraj. Eventually they threatened war unless Faridun agreed to exile Iraj to a realm as remote as their own. Faridun replied sorrowly to Salm and Tur, beseeching them to remain peaceful and to love their brother, Iraj, who bore the letter to them. When the brothers received this message of peace and love, they blustered with rage. Tur hoisted his solid gold throne in the air and brought it crashing down on the head of Iraj. Still conscious, Iraj evoked God's name and sued for mercy. But Tur plunged his dagger into his brother's heart and finished the deed by severing the prince's head. The embalmed head was then dispatched to Faridun with a message, "Here is your crowning glory!" S. R. C.

Wailing choruses of women, cruelly geometric ornament, and a pinnacle of rock, upper left, red as blood, contribute to the murderous atmosphere of this miniature. Probably later than the same artist's *Faridun Crosses the River Dijla* (no. 12), but earlier than *The Death of Zuhhak* (no 13), it recalls them both, as well as *The Court of Gayumars* (no. 8). Why, one wonders, were several passages barely colored in? Was the subject distasteful to the Shah, who did not care to see it in greater detail? Or does it represent a stage beyond which Sultan-Muhammad felt no need to go, a stage at which a younger man, such as Mir Sayyid-'Ali, might have been called in to complete the picture? Whatever the answer, it is a brilliant and moving miniature; and the bold arrangement of white tents seems to have inspired the design of Mir Sayyid-'Ali's *Majnun Brought in Chains by the Old Woman to Layla's Tent* in the *Quintet* (no. 61).

دوان خون از آن چهر ارغوان
شد آن نامور شهریار جهان
سر تاجور زان تن پیلوار
بخنجر جدا کرد و برگشت کار
جهانا بپروردیش در کنار
وز آن پس ندادی بجان زینهار

16. *Zal is Sighted by a Caravan*

From Shah Tahmasp's BOOK OF KINGS, folio 62 verso
Probably by 'Abd ul-'Aziz, closely directed by Sultan-Muhammad

Ca. 1525
310 x 172 mm. (miniature only)
Private Collector

Sam, the guardian of Faridun's great-grandson and the greatest paladin in Iran, ruled the eastern provinces of Sistan and Zabulistan as the Shah's vassal. After many childless years Sam finally fathered a son. Endowed with good health and a fine complexion, the boy had one major flaw—totally white hair. When Sam observed this, he despaired and banished the boy, named Zal, to almost certain death on Mount Alburz.

The abandoned babe wailed for a day and a night until a magical bird, the Simurgh, spied him in her flight. She grasped Zal in her talons and carried him off to her nest, where she reared him with her own young. Occasionally caravans passed far below and people caught sight of the striking-looking child in the Simurgh's aerie. Rumors spread of the white-haired child living atop a mountain crag too high to climb; and at last the strange news reached Sam himself. S. R. C.

Dust-Muhammad's Preface refers to the "creative works" that Sultan-Muhammad "painted and sketched." Doubtless, this miniature belongs to the second category. For while none of its color can be ascribed to the great master, it is one of the most arresting lesser pictures in the *Shahnama* and could not have come into being without Sultan-Muhammad's deep involvement.[1] The smoldering mood, sinuous wiggle of forms, and odd profile faces, with strongly protruding brows, all point to an artist we have identified with slight hesitation as 'Abd ul-'Aziz.[2] We trace his work from about 1525 through the more naturalistic phase of the *Quintet* (to which he did not contribute) and into the years of the Freer Jami of 1556–1565. Although his later miniatures are calmer, with few recollections of the expressive turbulence seen here, his temperament seems to have been sensual and torrid, comparable perhaps to that of the alluring Simurgh shown here bringing the day's catch to Zal and her own young. Although Sadiki Bek, who grew up in Tabriz in the 1540s, refers to 'Abd ul-'Aziz as a young pupil of Bihzad, adding that "he was an artist of many talents . . . particularly good at ornamentation," his early pictures for the *Shahnama* reveal him as a follower of Sultan-Muhammad, with a strong taste for Turkman art.

1. This miniature was such a success that it was followed immediately by *Sam Comes to Mount Alburz* (folio 63 verso) by the same artist. It is now in the Museum für Islamisch Kunst, Dahlem. See Welch, *A King's Book of Kings*, pp. 124–127.

2. For a color plate of this miniature, see Welch, *Persian Painting*, pl. 8.

شکاری که نازکتر آن برگزید
که بی شیر مهمان همی خون مزید
بدین گونه تا روزگار دراز
براورد و دارنده بگشاد راز
جوان کودک خرد پرمایه گشت
بران کوه بر کاروانها گذشت
یکی مرد شد چون یکی زاد سرو
برش کوه سیم و میانش چو غرو
نشانش پراکنده شد در جهان
بد و نیک هرگز نماند نهان
بسام نریمان رسید آگهی
ازان نیک پی پور با فرهی

17. Sam Returns from Mount Alburz with His Son Zal

From Shah Tahmasp's BOOK OF KINGS, folio 64 verso
Attributable to Qadimi, closely directed by Sultan-Muhammad

Ca. 1525
354 x 168 mm. (miniature only)
Private Collector

One night Sam dreamed a noble horseman dashed out of the land of Hind to announce that his son lived. Sam's magi interpreted this to mean God had saved Zal despite Sam's abandonment. The humbled paladin set out at once for Mount Alburz to retrieve his son.

Sam saw the Simurgh's nest from the foot of the mountain, but could not scale the cliff. The bird understood Sam's mission and carried the boy to his father, but first she gave Zal one of her plumes, telling him to burn it if he ever needed her.

Sam greeted his son like a true prince, recognizing his beauty and nobility. Reunited, Sam and Zal rode home in triumph. S. R. C.

Qadimi, too, excelled under the eye of Sultan-Muhammad; here he works over a design sketched by that great master. "Primitive" compared to Aqa-Mirak or Mir Musavvir, he compensates with earthy gusto, flashes of ribald humor, and heartfelt sympathy. The Simurgh's sad flight back to her nest after leaving Zal is one of the more tearful moments in the manuscript. The miniature is also festive with panoply, and explodes into the upper margin.

Qadimi's highly individual style, known from inscribed works in Istanbul[1], retains much of the powerful but raw Turkman idiom of his birthplace, Gilan.[2] Under Sultan-Muhammad, he modified such Gilani ways as painting overly large heads with deep wrinkles. But, in the words of Dust-Muhammad, "He holds to the priority of generic-type over individual form; for him, in poetry as in painting, everything must conform to that." Qazi Ahmad reinforces this view of Qadimi when he describes him as "an *abdal* type of person," using a word, still current in Turkish, meaning "bumpkin."

1. Both are reproduced in Armenag Beg Sakisian, *La Miniature persane du XIIe au XVIIe siècle* (Paris and Brussels: G. Van Oest, 1929) Figs. 64, 175.

2. See Robinson, et. al., *The Keir Collection*, no. III, pp. 128–131, color pls. 15–17.

نشستش را یکی پهلوانی قبای | بپوشید و از کوه بگزارد پای
فرود آمد از کوه و بالای خواست | همان جامهٔ خسروآرای خواست
سپه یکسره پیش سام آمدند | گشاده دل و شادکام آمدند
تبیره زنان پیش بردند پیل | برآمد یکی گرد چون کوه نیل
خروشیدن کوس با کرّه نای | همان زنگ زرّین و هندی درای
سواران همه نعره برداشتند | بدان خرّمی روز بگذاشتند

بشادی بشهر اندرون آمدند
ابا پهلوانی فزون آمدند

18. *Qaran Slays Barman*

From Shah Tahmasp's BOOK OF KINGS, folio 102 verso
Attributable to Sultan-Muhammad, assisted by Mir Sayyid-'Ali

Ca. 1530–35
306 x 223 mm. (miniature only)
Lent anonymously

The murder of Iraj incited hostilities between Iran and Turan that continued for centuries. To avenge one of their defeats by the Iranians, Afrasiyab and Barman, descendants of Tur, raised a huge army for the invasion of Iran. Although the weakling Iranian Shah tried to flee, the fortress in which he and his army took refuge soon came under Turanian siege.

Qaran, the brother of a slain Iranian warrior, desired to seek vengeance and to insure the safety of the inner provinces of Iran. Against the Shah's will he led a nocturnal mission behind Turanian lines. Soon after advancing into enemy territory Qaran caught sight of Barman, his brother's murderer. At once he gave chase. Closing in on his prey, Qaran speared him through the waist. Next he hacked off his victim's head and dangled it from his saddlebow. The members of his party joined in the fray and routed the Turanians under Barman's command. Nonetheless, the Shah and those who had remained with him met an inglorious fate. While trying to escape, they fell one by one into the hands of Afrasiyab's soldiers. S. R. C.

A glowing, peacock-hued palette—among the most original in the entire manuscript—makes this one of the memorable battle scenes in Iranian art,[1] along with another in Edinburgh, from Shah Tahmasp's *Quintet* (no. 66). Similarities between the two are to be expected, for Mir Sayyid-'Ali, the extraordinarily talented and meticulous young master who helped finish this one, was solely responsible for the other. Evidently his weeks or months bent over this picture were instructive. Several figures and horsemen were re-employed. He did not, however, master his mentor's knack for communicating feel and and sound; and with this distinction in mind one can survey this battle group by group to differentiate the artists' hands. Qaran spears Barman, for instance, in dispassionate silence, and their horses seem equally unmoved. On the other hand, we can hear and empathize with the fleshy triad of horses, right foreground, who gallop provocatively out of the picture.

1. For color reproductions, see Welch, *A King's Book of Kings*, pp. 137, 138.

ازو قارن رزم زن خسته بود
بخون برادر کمر بسته بود
برآویخت چون شیر با بارمان
بسوی چاره جستن ندادش امان

یکی نیزه زد بر کمربند او
که بگسست بنیاد و پیوند او
فرود آمد و سر بریدش ز تن
برآویخت از زین کو انجمن

بفرمود قارن بیاران خود
که ای نامداران و گردان خود
برآرید از این نابکاران دمار
که برگشته بخت‌اند و بد روزگار

بکشتند چندی ز توران سپاه
به بستند دیگر بسی کینه خواه
برفتند نزدیک افراسیاب
غمین گشته از رزم و دل پرشتاب

وزانسو که بد شاه نوذر بجای
در اندیشه بد تا چه آرد خدای
چو آگاه شد نامور پادشاه
که قارن گذر کرد از آن رزمگاه

غمی گشت و لشکر همه برگرفت
چو تیر از پس روی بنهاد و رفت
همی خواست کز روز بد بگذرد
سپهرش مگر زیر پی بسپرد

چنین گفت روشن دلی تیز هوش
پسر را که گر شاهیی پند گوش
ز تقدیر کس نگذرد بی‌گمان
اگر خود بپرد بسوی آسمان

چنین است گردون ناپایدار
که با کس نباشد همی سازگار
اگر شهریار است اگر پاسبان
چو روزش سر آمد نبخشد امان

چو افراسیاب آگهی یافت زو
که سوی بیابان نهان کرد رو
سپاه انجمن کرد و پویان برفت
دمان از پس شاه جویان برفت

19. *Rustam Finds Kay Qubad*

From Shah Tahmasp's BOOK OF KINGS, folio 110 verso
Attributable to Aqa-Mirak

Ca. 1530
356 x 218 mm. (miniature only)
Lent anonymously

Following the Turanian invasion and years of strife and famine, Zal and his giant son Rustam, Iran's legendary hero, pledged to find a rightful heir to the Iranian throne. Luckily, a magus informed Zal that Kay Qubad, a legitimate descendant of Faridun, lived on Mount Alburz. Without delay Zal dispatched Rustam and his newly acquired horse, Rakhsh, to seek him out. As Rustam neared Mount Alburz he entered a lush grove, and, in the shade by a sparkling stream, he spied a throne on which sat a beautiful young man surrounded by attendants. Led before the throne, Rustam explained his mission to the moon-like youth. The prince smiled and introduced himself as Kay Qubad. Rustam bowed in deference to the future Shah as the musicians began to intone their melodies. S.R.C.

Painting over two hundred and fifty miniatures for a single manuscript must have been a fearful challenge, even to Shah Tahmasp's ambitious and enthusiastic artists. Over the years of the project, therefore, the major artists devised ways of painting more quickly, if possible without sacrificing aesthetic standards. Sultan-Muhammad and Mir Musavvir found adept followers, for whom they provided guidance, sometimes to the point of making detailed sketches to be colored. Inasmuch as Sultan-Muhammad's earlier, pre-Bihzadian, miniatures such as *Rustam Sleeping* (no. 2), were dashingly sketchy, he was apparently used to working in this quicker vein, and some of his liveliest pictures for the early phase of the project are of this sort. Later, to please Shah Tahmasp's increasingly refined taste, he employed such young masters as Mir Sayyid-'Ali as assistants. Aqa-Mirak also assigned Mir Sayyid-'Ali to such tasks; and he also guided lesser painters as well. But his own pictures, stemming from the meticulously hard-edged tradition of Bihzad and Shaykh-Zadeh (see no. 42), required much time; moreover, his later miniatures, such as *Faridun in the Guise of a Dragon* (no. 14) took even longer to paint than his broader, simpler and earlier ones, of which *Bizhan Forces Farud to Flee* (no. 22) is the outstanding example. *Rustam Finds Kay Qubad*[1] is the key transitional picture linking Aqa-Mirak's powerful, richly colored, broad style to his later, less vivid, subtler, more polished manner. Daringly designed, with a mountainscape looming into the margin, it is also innovatively sunlit, and its characterizations anticipate yet more penetrating portraiture to come.

1. For color reproductions, see Welch, *A King's Book of Kings*, pp. 145, 146.

بکوی که کردان نرا حواستند
بشادی جهان پار اپستند
زکفتار رستم دلیر جوان
بخندید وکفتش که ای پهلوان
زتخم فریدون منم کیقباد
پدر بر پدر نام دارم بیاد
نشان ار توانی ودانی ورا
دهی وبشاهی رپسانی ورا
جو بشنید رستم فرو برد سر
بخدمت فرود آمد از تخت زر

20. *Rustam and the "Seven" Champions Hunt in Turan*

From Shah Tahmasp's BOOK OF KINGS, folio 135 verso
Attributable to Mir Sayyid-'Ali

Ca. 1530
264 x 211 mm. (miniature only)
Lent by Arthur A. Houghton, Jr.

When Rustam was not battling demons or armies on behalf of Kay Ka'us, he enjoyed his favorite pastimes—hunting and feasting. During one peaceful interlude, Rustam invited the "Seven" Champions (who really numbered twelve) to a splendid feast. As the men sat drinking, one proposed a hunt at the expense of Afrasiyab, the Turanian Shah. All agreed to it; and, after crossing the River Shahd, Rustam and the "Seven" slaughtered scores of deer, sheep and other beasts which accumulated in piles higher than the Iranian tents. When the hunters had exhausted the supply of game on the ground, they raised their bows toward the sky and showered the earth with slain fowl. The Champions kept up their hunting and feasting for a week, even after learning that Afrasiyab was leading an army of thirty thousand men in their direction. Since each Champion knew he was equal to five hundred Turanians, why stop drinking toasts and arm for battle until the Turanians actually appeared on the horizon? Fortunately, on this occasion Iranian pride was justified. S. R. C.

One of the fascinations of the Houghton *Shahnama* is the presence among its illustrations of early work by the second generation of Safavid artists, such as Mir Sayyid-'Ali. Already in this picture from his late adolescence, one senses pride of accomplishment, in his jewel-like technique, design of ornament, and analytical studies of still life. Combining close observation of nature with gracefully curving abstract forms—a talent learned from his father—he also gained much from his apprenticeship to Sultan-Muhammad and Aqa-Mirak. Compare, for instance, the lion in the left foreground with that in *Faridun Crosses the River Dijla* (no. 12). Although here the treatment of rocks, the slightly puffy faces with unfocusing eyes, and the ornament identify Mir Sayyid-'Ali's hand, the presence of a particular hook-nosed, weak-chinned man at the upper right confirms the attribution. For this unique characterization, shown at several stages of life, appears frequently in Mir Sayyid-'Ali's Tabriz miniatures, and is a virtual signature.

برفتند با یوز و بازان و مهد
گرازان و تازان تا رود شهد
دگر سو سر خسرو پابانش پش
گلگشته بر دشت آهو وشیش
همه دشت پر خرگه و خیمه گشت
زانبوه آهو پراسیمه گشت
ز درنده شیران زمین شد تهی
بپرنده مرغان رسید آگهی
تلی مرغ هر سوی نخچیر بود
اگر کشته گر خسته تیر بود
ببودند گردان چنین یکزمان
بران دشت روشن دل و شادمان
وزان هفته زین گونه با می بدست
ببودند شادان دل و می پرست
بهشتم تهمتن بیامد بگاه
یکی رای شایسته زد با سپاه

21. *Siyavush and Afrasiyab in the Hunting Field*

From Shah Tahmasp's BOOK OF KINGS, folio 182 verso
Probably by Qasim Son of 'Ali, supervised by Mir Musavvir

Ca. 1525–30
219 x 173 mm. (miniature only)
Lent by Arthur A. Houghton, Jr.

To Kay Ka'us and one of his wives, a Turanian princess, was born a son named Siyavush. As a grown man, Siyavush commanded the Iranian army in its defence of Balkh against the invading armies of Turan. When Afrasiyab sued for peace, Siyavush and his co-commandant Rustam accepted the bid, much to the consternation of Kay Ka'us, who did not trust the Turanian. Berated by Kay Ka'us, Rustam sulkingly returned to Zabulistan while Siyavush chose self-exile in Turan, where Afrasiyab greeted him as an honored guest with feasts and sporting events.

Having bewildered the Turanians with his skill at polo and archery, Siyavush dazzled them again at the hunt. In one day of hunting he cleaved an onager into two perfectly equal halves and amassed heaps of game. While Afrasiyab was truly delighted with his guest's prowess, jealous favorites at court schemed against him. Their evil plans took time to mature, however, and over the next year Afrasiyab and Siyavush became inseparable companions. S. R. C.

The Shah's painting studios included humbler men as well as outstanding masters. Some, like Qadimi and 'Abd al-Aziz, worked in styles so individual that they can be recognized even when aided by more powerful artists. The painter of this miniature is more difficult to identify. Chameleon-like, he took on the ways of his mentors. When working with Sultan-Muhammad, he aped him; and when assisting Mir Musavvir, he conformed to the latter's mellifluous artistic personality. Occasionally, as here in his most successful picture, he pieced together elements from both senior masters, and devised a lively, if archaic, composition of considerable originality. Sam Mirza, a brother of the Shah, wrote that Qasim son of 'Ali came from Shiraz, assigned him about the same rank as Qadimi, and added that he died young, in 1540/41. Our identification is based upon the similarity between many of his other pictures painted for the *Shahnama* in collaboration with Mir Musavvir, and signed work in a copy of the *Ahsan ul-Kibar* in the State Public Library, Leningrad.[1]

1. Dorn 312. See O. F. Akimushkin and A. A. Ivanov, *Persidskie miniaturī XIV–XVII vv* (Moscow: Nauka, 1968) pp. 21–22, 36–37; pls. 34–36.

شکار کردن سیاوش
بیک جو ز یکسو گران سر نبود
بگفتند یکسر همه انجمن
باواز گفتند با یکدگر
همه نام ما اندر آمد بتنگ
بهر جایگه بر یکی توده کرد
سزد گر بپا زیم با شاه جنگ
سپه را ز نخچیر آسوده کرد
بغار و بکوه و بهامون بتاخت
نظاره شد و لشکر و شاه زو
که اینت سرافراز و شمشیرزن
که ما را بد آمد ز ایران سپر
بتیر و بشمشیر و نیزه بساخت
وز انجایگه سوی ایوان شاه
همه شاد دل برگرفتند راه

22. *Bizhan Forces Farud to Flee*

From Shah Tahmasp's BOOK OF KINGS, folio 234 recto
Attributable to Aqa-Mirak

Ca. 1530
247 x 236 mm. (miniature only)
Private Collector

Before his assassination, Siyavush had married two wives. To one a son Farud was born, while the other gave birth to Kay Khusraw, the future Iranian Shah. Shortly after Kay Khusraw acceded to the throne, Iran resumed its war with Turan. Against Kay Khusraw's orders, his commander in chief, Tus, led the army past the fortress of Farud and his mother. Farud came out to offer his assistance in the war, but Tus tragically disregarded his overtures and ordered him killed.

In self defence Farud was forced to humiliate and kill soldier after soldier until finally young Bizhan came forth to avenge those who had fallen. Undaunted by the death of his horse, Bizhan pressed forward after Farud. Although Farud escaped Bizhan's first attack, that night in a surprise foray the Iranian army decimated Farud's forces. Bizhan then dealt a death blow to Farud, who barely reached his castle door before expiring. S. R. C.

چو بیژن همی برنگشت از فرود
سپر بر درید و زره را بتافت
فرود گرانمایه زو بازگشت
به برگستوان بر زد و کرد چاک
گرانمایه اسپ اندر آمد به خاک
فرود اندران کار تیزی نمود
از آن تیر بیژن بسستی نتافت
همه باره در زیر آوار گشت
یکی تیر دیگر بینداخت شیر
از آن تند بالا چو سر برکشید
دوان بیژن آمد سوی پشت او
سپر بر سر آورد گرد دلیر
برد دست و تیغ از میان برکشید
یکی تیغ بد تیز در مشت او
خروشید بیژن که ای نامدار
پیامد بر طوس ازان رزمگاه
نه مرد پیاده دلیر و سوار
چنین گفت کای پهلوان سپاه
بدر بند حصن اندر آمد فرود
ز باره فراوان بباریدسنگ
چنین بازگشتی و شرمت نبود
سزد گر برزم چنین یک دلیر
دلیران در دژ ببستند زود
بدانست کان نیست جای درنگ
دریغ آن دل و نام جنگی فرود
شود نامبردار یک دست شیر

Of all Shah Tahmasp's artists, Aqa-Mirak was the one who derived most joy from painting. He was also the most reckless in setting himself seemingly impossible artistic challenges—a characteristic that brings to mind an aspect of his life recorded by Qazi Ahmad, who wrote that "with carefree abandon he was constantly in love," adding that "he was congenial in society, a man wise in his ways." His compositions are airily free and organic, laced together by such trickling lines as the horizon here or the falling water in *Faridun Tests His Sons* (no. 14). Sensitive to growing plants, he enjoyed their silhouettes. His most original compositional scheme was a seemingly random arrangement of shapes across the picture, comparable to the miscellaneous objects jugglers toss into the air. And like the jugglers, Aqa-Mirak balanced his scattered horses, trees, or boulders in spontaneous harmony. He avoided symmetry; and even his superbly ornamental clumps of leaves, flowers, and stones are dynamic. Invariably, his people behave with courtly formality, however; and one senses that the artist's special joy, other than being in love, was the release he found in such passages as the rocks here, a fluidly brushed, dazzlingly jewel-like, visionary ecstasy (color detail, p. 81).

OPPOSITE PAGE: Detail of no. 22.

یکی جنگ با پشن افگند پی
که این دشت جنگست یا جای می
سراسیمه شد پشت از دار و گیر
بر آمد یکی ابر بارانش تیر
سپیده چو برزد سر از برج شیر
بلشکر نگه کرد گیو دلیر
همه رزمگه سر بسر کشته دید
زمین سر بسر چون گل آغشته دید
همی کرد گودرز هر سو نگاه
ز دشمن نفرود هر دم سپاه
سپاه اندر آمد بگرد سپاه
یکی بانگ برخاست از رزمگاه
بزیر سر مست بالین نرم
ز بر تیغ و شمشیر و گوپال گرم
همه دشت از ایرانیان کشته دید
ز لشکر دلیران و مردان بد
دریده درفش و نگون کرده کوس
رخ زندگان گشته چون آبنوس
بدان اندکی بر کشیدند نخ
سپاهی ز زنگان چو مور و ملخ
پدر بی پسر شد پسر بی پدر
همه لشکر گشن زیر و زبر
چنین آمد این گنبد تیزگرد
گهی شادمانی دهد گاه درد

23. *The Drunken Iranian Camp Attacked at Night*

From Shah Tahmasp's BOOK OF KINGS, folio 241 recto
Attributable to Qadimi

Ca. 1530
259 x 224 mm. (miniature only)
Lent by The Metropolitan Museum of Art, Gift of Arthur A. Houghton, Jr., 1970 (1970.301.36)

Following the death of Farud, the Iranian army swept across Turan. Tus and his men successfully stormed the fortress at Girawgird and put the renowned paladin Tazhav to flight. As the Turanians mobilized a vast army under the command of Piran, the Iranian army celebrated its victory at the castle of Girawgird. Piran soon learned from his spies that the Iranians in their drunken revelry had posted no guards, and with an army of thirty thousand men he burst upon the unsuspecting Iranians in the dead of night. Giv first heard the cries of the enemy but failed to raise the Iranians from their stupor. Turanians swooped down, daggers unsheathed, upon their drunken victims. The few Iranians who could staggered from the camp, deserting their wounded, and stumbled forward in the direction of the River Kasa. When they finally regrouped in the mountains, only one third of the Iranian army was found to have survived. S. R. C.

If *Qaran Slays Barman* (no. 18) is the grandest battle scene in the *Shahnama*, this is the funniest.[1] In it, broken-nosed, craggy-jawed veterans and cocksure young firebrands slash, stab, and batter one another with unflinching, if alcoholic, bravery. The subject must have been sympathetic to Qadimi, "The Veteran," who probably had experienced such melees, and surely knew the mixed blessings of wine. Inspired here, he surpassed his usual limits, presumably urged on by Sultan-Muhammad, whose range of moods included such burlesquery. Over the years of the *Shahnama* project, Qadimi's mastery of drawing and painting gained refinement. Although his buffoonery was not welcome, it seems, in the Shah's *Quintet*, Sultan Ibrahim Mirza apparently admired Qadimi's barracks humor, which reappears, albeit in up to date guise, in miniatures for the Freer Jami.[2]

1. For color reproductions, see Welch, *A King's Book of Kings*, pp. 156, 158.

2. See Dickson and Welch, *The Houghton Shahnameh*, figs. 263–265.

24. *The Combat of Rustam and Shangul*

From Shah Tahmasp's BOOK OF KINGS, folio 279 verso
Attributable to Aqa-Mirak

Ca. 1530
296 x 258 mm. (miniature only)
Lent by Arthur A. Houghton, Jr.

Defeated in the First War in Revenge of Siyavush, the Iranians appeared to be similarly fated at the Battle of Mount Hamavan in the Second War. The Turanian forces were joined by several formidable allies—the Khaqan of Chin, Kamus of Kashan, and Shangul Shah of Hind. Only Rustam could save the day.

Luckily, he arrived at Mount Hamavan and immediately set about slaying Turanian heroes. As the Battle of Mount Hamavan entered its fourth and final day, Shangul Shah of Hind rode into the midst of the bloody fray roaring challenges at Rustam. The Iranian champion lunged at the Indian, and in a flash Rustam's horse Rakhsh was trampling Shangul, who was spared only when a horde of soldiers rushed Rustam. They dragged the Shah of Hind back to camp where he exclaimed to the Khaqan of Chin, "No mere man is Rustam. . . . He comes raging at you like a rampaging elephant rearing atop a heaving mountainside. . . ." S.R.C.

While Rustam lifts Shangul from his saddle in another of Aqa-Mirak's boldly simplified compositions, our attention is drawn to the rocks at the center of the page, which suggest a gathering of strange people and animals. Faces turn and prattle, gape, or complain with far more animation than the sixteen battle-bent warriors who frame them. As usual in Aqa Mirak's series of broadly treated pictures (see also nos. 22, 29, and 36), the colors are immaculate in tone, and the clear but muted landscape evokes areas near his native Isfahan. Inasmuch as Aqa-Mirak was more concerned than Shah Tahmasp's other artists with the quality of pigments, it is not surprising that he was charged with the purchase of such materials for the royal ateliers.

آمدن شنگل هند
و رزم کردن با رستم

گزارشه گیتی بران سان بود
بغرید شنگل به پیش سپاه
بپرسیم کاین مرد سگزی کجاست
چو آواز شنگل برستم رسید
که بیگانه زان بزرگ انجمن
بر شنگل آمد باواز گفت
نگه کن که سگزی کنون مرگ تست
یکی نیزه زد بر گرفتش ز زین
نگونسار کرد و بزد بر زمین

ز شنگل نگه کرد و او را بدید
دلیری کند رزم جوید همین
که ای بدنژاد فرومایه جفت
کفن بی گمان جوشن و ترگ تست

چنین گفت کز گرد کار جهان
نه سقلاب مانم بدیشان نه هند
مرا نام رستم کند زال زر
همی گشت با او بآوردگاه

یکی خوار و دیگرش آسان بود
منم گفت گرد افکن و رزم خواه
یکی گرد خواهم برو دست را
نجستم جز این آشکار و نهان
نه شمشیر رومی نه چینی پرند
تو سگزی چرا خوانی ای بدگهر
میان وصف برکشیده سپاه

بر و بر گذر کرد و او را نخست
به شمشیر برد آن زمان شیر دست

برون شد بنخچیر چون نره شیر
کمندی بدست اژدهای بزیر
بدشتی که جا داشت چوپان گله
بدانجا گذر داشت گور یله

سه روزش همی جست از آن مرغزار
همی کرد برگرد اسپان شکار
چهارم بدیدش گرازان بدشت
چو باد شمالی برو برگذشت

درخشنده زرین یکی باره بود
بچرم اندرون زشت بتیاره بود
برانگیخت رستم تکاور ز جای
چو تنگ اندر آمد دگر شد برای

چنین گفت کین را بباید فکند
بباید گرفتن بخم کمند
نبایدش کردن بنخچیر تباه
بر بینیانش زنده برم نزد شاه

بینداخت رستم کیانی کمند
همی خواست کارد سرش را ببند

25. Rustam Pursues Akvan the Onager Div

From Shah Tahmasp's BOOK OF KINGS, folio 294 recto
Attributable to Muzaffar-'Ali

Ca. 1530–35
268 x 173 mm. (miniature only)
Private Collection

A herdsman complained one day to Kay Khusraw that a particularly vicious onager was attacking the horses in his care. From the description of its golden hide and its lair near a mysterious spring, Kay Khusraw suspected that the wild ass was a new form of Akvan, a wicked and destructive div. Such was the div's power that only Rustam possessed the strength necessary to rid the world of it. At Kay Khusraw's request Rustam mounted Rakhsh and set off to track down Akvan. After searching for three days, Rustam spotted the golden onager galloping across the plain. Rustam and Rakhsh gave chase, but as the noose of Rustam's lasso touched Akvan's neck, the onager vanished into thin air.

For days Rustam and Rakhsh sought the invisible div. Finally, exhausted, Rustam lay down by a gurgling spring and fell asleep. Unknowingly Rustam had chosen Akvan's lair as his resting place. While he slept, the evil div tunneled underneath him and lifted him high in the air. Rustam awoke to Akvan's question, "Do I hurl you onto the mountains or do I heave you into the sea?" Although Rustam preferred the sea, he understood the workings of the div's mind and begged, "Not the sea!" In an instant Rustam found himself in the deep. Fighting off sharks with one arm, he swam ashore.

S. R. C.

One of the most lyrical and buoyant designs in Safavid painting, this picture is also Muzaffar-'Ali's outstanding contribution to the *Shahnama*. Everything from horses to trees and tufts of grass fairly bounds off the page, while the onager-div roars away from Rustam, lent extra power by the wavy line between him and his pursuer.[1]

According to Sadiki, the late sixteenth-century artist, wanderer, and man of letters who was his pupil, Muzaffar-'Ali was admirable in character as in his art—"an illuminated man, morally upright. . . . profoundly humane." A grand-nephew of Bihzad, he was the son of the painter Haydar-'Ali. His family came from Turbat, between Herat and Mashhad. Sadiki also tells us that he was a fine calligrapher and excellent at chess. He died soon after Shah Tahmasp in 1576.

Although he was slower to develop as a craftsman than his contemporaries Mir Sayyid-'Ali and Mirza-'Ali, in his best work, such as this miniature, spirit and charm compensate for the lack of exquisite finish. His special qualities were intuitive, and enabled him to paint cavorting animals thinly and quickly, with a vivacity stemming from inner understanding rather than outer observation. Unlike Mir Sayyid-'Ali, whose life-like proportions and textures imply that he drew from nature, and whose methods were slow and arduous, Muzaffar-'Ali worked rapidly with pure joy.

1. For color reproductions, see Welch, *A King's Book of Kings*, pp. 160, 163.

26. Rustam Recovers Rakhsh from Afrasiyab's Herds

From Shah Tahmasp's BOOK OF KINGS, folio 295 recto
Attributable to Mirza-'Ali

Ca. 1530–35
353 x 280 mm. (miniature only)
Lent by Arthur A. Houghton, Jr.

While Rustam was being tossed into the sea by Akvan, his horse Rakhsh wandered away from Akvan's lair. Rustam tracked Rakhsh to a meadow and found him prancing in the midst of a herd of horses. The Hero lassoed him and rode off, followed by the entire herd. As luck would have it, the herd belonged to Afrasiyab, the Turanian Shah, to whom the alarmed herdsman immediately sent word of disaster.

By chance, on the very day that Rustam led Afrasiyab's herd away, the most prominent paladins of Turan were celebrating the annual inspection of the royal stud farms. When they heard the news, they hotly pursued Rustam on Afrasiyab's war elephants and on foot. The Iranian hero slew one hundred Turanians, causing Afrasiyab and his men to flee in terror. On returning to Iran Rustam again visited Akvan's lair. This time he caught the div, bashed in his brains and chopped off his head. With Akvan's head and Afrasiyab's horses in tow, Rustam returned to a hero's welcome at the court of Kay Khusraw. S. R. C.

Courtiers, not rustics or heros, were Mirza-'Ali's preferred subjects; and horses were never his specialty. But here, perhaps goaded on by Muzaffar-'Ali's example in the preceding folio, he proved the uncanny range of his abilities. Indeed, if his interests were primarily indoor, and human behavior interested him far more than untamed nature, he could paint anything and everything. Here, he made more of the setting than of the action, and concentrated his attention on the gnarled, mossy rocks and the massive tree that holds them in a curious embrace. While painting the creamy twists of cloud, he seems to have been thinking of his father Sultan-Muhammad's configurations of witches and dragons.

27. *The First "Joust of the Rooks:" Fariburz Against Kalbad*

From Shah Tahmasp's BOOK OF KINGS, folio 341 verso
Attributable to Shaykh-Muhammad

Ca. 1540
220 x 172 mm. (miniature only)
Lent by Arthur A. Houghton, Jr.

In yet another resumption of hostilities between Turan and Iran the two sides reached a stalemate. Piran, the Turanian commander, and Gudarz, his Iranian counterpart, resolved to seek victory through a series of individual jousts. Each side would be represented by the commanders and ten champions called rooks. Whichever team won the eleven-round contest would be the victor of the war.

Having selected their contestants, the rival commanders agreed upon a battle plain overlooked by two hills—one for Iran and one for Turan. Although the site was remote, the armies would learn the results of the matches by seeing the victor's standard on the mound of his side.

In the first joust Prince Fariburz, son of Kay Ka'us, met Kalbud, brother of Piran. Although Fariburz missed Kalbud with his arrows, he immediately drew his sword and cleaved his foe in two from neck to waist. Removing Kalbad's armor, he lashed him to his mount. Atop the Iranian mound he hailed his commander, Gudarz, and his Shah. Seemingly, this first match set the tone for those that followed. Each Iranian champion in turn routed his opponent. S. R. C.

Painted on heavier, creamier paper than the original illustrations to the *Shahnama*, this miniature and Dust-Muhammad's *Haftvad and the Worm* (no. 31) must have been inserted after the manuscript's completion. On the basis of a signed miniature of a camel with its keeper in a landscape strikingly similar to this one, we assigned it to Shaykh-Muhammad. In this, his earliest known picture, his temperament is already definable. Spiky trees, pointed, rodent-like rocks, and exceptionally realistic wounds, gushing with blood, bespeak a militant spirit. His aggressiveness, however, combines with delicacy, as can be seen in the surgical incisiveness of outlining. His precocious gifts as a portraitist are also apparent. Fariburz and Kalbad both impress us as individuals. Like the other miniatures of this manuscript illustrating the series of jousts, Shaykh-Muhammad's is consciously archaistic, seemingly derived from a battle by Bihzad from which Shaykh-Muhammad adapted the central figures.[1] Inasmuch as Bihzad was the master of Dust-Muhammad, who, in turn, is known to have taught Shaykh-Muhammad, this derivation is peculiarly fitting. In the Bihzadian tradition, Shaykh-Muhammad applied pigments in heavy, leathery layers, prone to developing craquelure. Unlike Dust-Muhammad, he was a patient, highly-skilled craftsman, whose services as a finisher of miniatures would have been invaluable to his master.[2]

Inscribed

on Fariburz' banner at right, and repeated on the pennant of his helmet
O God! O Muhammad! O 'Ali!

on illuminated chapter heading, serving here as a picture caption as well
The Killing of Kalbad at the Hands of Fariburz

1. See *Iskandar Defeats Dara*, folio 231 verso, from a Nizami in the British Library (Add. 25900); published in: Ivan V. Stchoukine, *Les Peintures des manuscrits safavis de 1502 à 1587* (Paris: Institut Français d'archéologie de Beyrouth, 1959) pl. 81.

2. For color reproductions, see Welch, *A King's Book of Kings*, pp. 165, 167.

کشته شدن کلباد بدست فریبرز
برآورد و زد تیغ بر گردنش
بدو نیمه شد تا کمرگه تنش
فرود آمد از اسپ و بگشاد بند
ز فتراک خویش آن کیانی کمند
که سالار ما باد پیروزگر
همه دشمن شاه خسته جگر

جهانجوی در پیش آن کوه بود
چو آن اژدها بر زراور بدید
چو از پیش زین اندر آویخت ترک
چو تنگ اندر آمد بر اژدها
سبک خنجر اندر دهانش نهاد
ز داور نیکی دهش کرد یاد

که آرام آن مار پتیوه بود
بدم سوی خویشش همی درکشید
بر او تیر بارید چون تگرگ
همی جست مرد جوان زو رها

همی ریخت زو زهر تا گشت سست
همه بخت مغزش بران سنگ سخت
خروشان بغلطید بر خاک بر
همی گفت لهراسب و فرخ زریر
ولیکن جز از رنج و سختی نبر

ز سر و بخون کوه یکسر بشست
ز اسب اندر آمد گو نیک بخت
به پیش خداوند پیروزگر
شدند از تن و جان گشتاسب سیر
ندیدیم بر جای تریاک زهر

بشمشیر زد آن زمان دست شیر
بکند از دهانش دو دندان بجست
که او داوش آن دستگاه بزرگ
بروشن روان و دل از زرناک
مگر زند کافی دها کرد کار

بزد تیز دندان بر آن خنجرش
همه تیغها شد بکام اندرش
بزد بر سر اژدهای دلیر
پس آنگه پیاده بیامد و تن بشست
بر آن گرگ و آن اژدهای سترگ
فکندم چنین اژدها را بخاک
به پیشم یکی روی آن شهریار

28. *Gushtasp Slays the Dragon of Mount Saqila*

From Shah Tahmasp's BOOK OF KINGS, folio 402 recto
Attributable to Mirza-'Ali

Ca. 1530–35
268 x 258 mm. (miniature only)
Private Collection

Gushtasp, the son of Shah Luhrasp, forsook the Iranian court for that of Rum. Disguised as Farrukhzad, he arrived at the court of Constantinople just as the Qaysar's daughter was choosing a husband. When the princess caught sight of Gushtasp, she desired only him as her mate; and they were married despite the Qaysar's disapproval. Because the Qaysar considered his first daughter's choice of a husband unsatisfactory, he announced that the suitors of his other two daughters would have to perform feats of daring before earning the princesses' hands.

The suitors of both daughters turned to Gushtasp to perform these feats in secret for them. First he killed a monster-wolf in the forest of Fasqun; then he set out to slay the ferocious dragon of Mount Saqila. With a specially designed dagger, the point of which was tempered in venom, Gushtasp lay in wait for the terrible creature. The minute the dragon spotted him, it began to suck in its breath and pull Gushtasp toward its maw. Undeterred, Gushtasp showered the dragon with arrows, then rammed his dagger down its throat. Once the monster's strength was sapped, Gushtasp hacked at its head with his sword and killed it. Fortunately, the truth of Gushtasp's valor became known to the Qaysar and the royal couple was restored to favor at the Rumi court. S.R.C.

Shot with light, this is Mirz-'Ali's most compelling image for the *Shahnama*. As usual in his work, the hero, horse, and dragon are shown in arrested motion, frozen at the perfect moment of equilibrium, so that they are simultaneously ornamental and dramatic. Trees and bushes vibrate, and the foreground sputters like breaking waves—lending urgency and monumentality to the action. Especially effective and innovative is the brilliant airiness produced by stark silhouetting against a light blue sky and dazzling gold ground. Few Safavid artists ever attempted such plein-air effects, which instill this picture with paradoxical naturalism and bring to earth the stuff of myths.[1]

1. For a color reproduction, see Welch, *Persian Painting*, pl. 9.

که چون باشد آغاز و فرجام جنگ — گرا پیش خواهد بد آنجا درنگ

بیامد خوش آن پیر جاماسپ را — بروی دژم گفت گشتاسپ را

که من خواستی کایزد دادگر — ندادی مرا این خرد وین هنر

مرا گر نبودی خرد شهریار — بکردی ز من بودنی خواستار

بگویم من این ور بگویم شاه — کند مر مرا شاه شاهان تباه

مگر با من از پیش پیمان کند — که نه بد کند خود نه فرمان کند

جهاندار گفتا بنام خدای — بدین و بنام آوری پاک رای

بجان زریر آن گرامی سوار — بجان گرانمایه اسفندیار

که نه سر کزت نیز دشمن کنم — نفرمایمت هیچ و نه من کنم

تو هرچه اندرین کار دانی بگوی — که تو چاره دانی و من چاره جوی

خردمند گفت ای گرانمایه شاه — همیشه بتو تازه باد اکلاه

بدان ای نبرده کو نامجوی — چو رزم آورد روی دشمن بروی

به پیش اندر آیند مردان مرد — هوا تیره گردد ز گرد نبرد

ازان زخم وان گرزهای گران — چنان زخم پولاد آهنگران

زبنده میازار و بنداز خشم — خنک آن کسی کو نه پیچد بخشم

بدانگه کجا بانگ و نعره زنند — تو گویی همی کوه را برکنند

جهان نیست آنگاه گشته کبود — زمین پر ز آتش هوا پر ز دود

29. *Jamasp Envisions the Disaster Awaiting Gushtasp*

From Shah Tahmasp's BOOK OF KINGS, folio 413 recto
Attributable to Aqa-Mirak

Ca. 1530–35
270 x 261 mm. (miniature only)
Lent by Arthur A. Houghton, Jr.

Gushtasp was reunited with his father Luhrasp, Shah of Iran, who later abdicated in favor of his son. During his reign Gushtasp converted to Zoroastrianism. Although Iran followed the Shah's example, the refusal of both Turan and Chin to accept the new faith touched off yet another war. Before the opposing armies clashed, Gushtasp sought a prediction of the battle's outcome from his chief minister, Jamasp. The trusted vizier described how the two sons of the Shah and his own son would be cut down. He foresaw a few Iranian victories followed by the death of the Iranian commander. Nonetheless, the tide would turn and Isfandiyar would avenge the Iranian dead, putting the Turanian shah to flight.

Distraught at this dreadful news, Gushtasp asked Jamasp whether by forbidding his sons to go to battle, he could stave off their fate. Jamasp replied, "Know that these are the workings of the Lord; nor is He an unjust tyrant. . . . What will be will be. Accept with joy what the just Lord gives!" The battle turned out as Jamasp had augured. In the aftermath of the Iranian victory, Jamasp was instated as chief magus and priest of a newly constructed Zoroastrian fire temple. S. R. C.

Unmistakably one of Aqa-Mirak's boldly simplified series for the *Shahnama*, the painting includes the delightful characterizations that lightly spoof those of Mir Musavvir. Such traces of personal interaction, when recognizable, lend humor and humanity to a manuscript which must have been an exasperating trial as well as a delight to patron and artists alike. In poking fun at the Mir's portrayals of stout courtiers, Aqa-Mirak was also commenting on the Shah's court, proof no doubt of his own privileged position within the inner circle. As a young man, Shah Tahmasp shared such private jocularity, as is proven by his own comically satirical portrait of his household staff.[1] If Aqa-Mirak enjoyed lampooning in this miniature, he also found deeper satisfactions in it. Once again the rocks released subconscious delights, and clusters of flowers were transformed into emblematic jewels.

1. See Welch, *A King's Book of Kings*, fig. 14.

30. *Ardashir and the Slave Girl Gulnar*

From Shah Tahmasp's BOOK OF KINGS, folio 516 verso
Attributable to Mir Musavvir

Dated 1527/28
206 x 171 mm. (miniature only)
Lent by Arthur A. Houghton, Jr.

As a young man, Ardashir, founder of the Sasanian dynasty, forsook the palace of his grandfather Babak at Istakhr to serve at the court of Ardavan, the Parthian king. Ardavan had ordered a special turret constructed in his palace at Ray, in which he kept his beloved concubine, the slave-girl Gulnar. One day Gulnar spied Ardashir from her pavilion and instantly fell in love with him. Her heart aflutter, Gulnar waited until the middle of the night and then lowered herself by a rope from her tower. She went to the bedside of Ardashir who awoke and was thrilled by her beauty. The lovers repeated their clandestine meetings often until Ardashir learned that his grandfather Babak had died, after appointing his son, not Ardashir, to succeed him. Compelled to return to Istakhr to claim the governorship by force, Ardashir stole off with Gulnar at his side. Enraged at the loss of his favorite, Ardavan pursued the couple; but they escaped to Fars unscathed. S. R. C.

The only date in Shah Tahmasp's *Shahnama* is in the architectural frieze of this particularly romantic miniature. Noting that the year corresponds to Shah Tahmasp's coming of age, Martin Bernard Dickson has suggested that the subject might not only illustrate Ardashir and Gulnar, but might allude to the first comparable experience in the life of the Shah. Whether or not it was sparked by an actual event, Mir Musavvir's picture is one of the most tender love scenes in Persianate painting.

Of the three senior masters responsible for the Houghton manuscript, Mir Musavvir is the gentlest and least assertive. To appreciate his art, one must contemplate the harmonies of his rounded arabesques, the doe-like beauty of his maidens, and his oddly personal colors—off greens, salmonish pinks, and almost turquoises. Even Mani, renowned in Iranian legend as a great painter, "in disgust and dismay threw his brush away," for he had been faced with the art of Mir Musavvir, "and artlessly he drew himself away." Like his son Mir Sayyid-'Ali, Mir Musavvir had a particular flair for transmuting everyday things into rapturously pleasing arrangements of pure color and form.[1]

1. For color reproductions, see Welch, *A King's Book of Kings*, pp. 169, 171.

که گلنار بد نام آن ماه روی — نگاری پر از گوهر و رنگ و بوی
بر اردوان همچو دستور بود — بگنج نهانیش گنجور بود

داستان اردشیر با گلنار

بر او بر گرامی‌تر از جان بدی — بدیدار او شاد و خندان بدی
جهان بد که روزی برآمد ببام — ازان خرمی گشته دل شاد کام
نگه کرد خندان لب اردشیر — جوان در دل ماه شد جای گیر
همی بود تا روز تاریک شد — سیه گشت شب صبح نزدیک شد
کمندی بدان کنگره در ببست — گره زد بر او چند ببسود دست
بگستاخی آمد ز باره فرود — همی داد نیکی دهش را درود
چو آمد خرامان بر اردشیر — پر از گوهر و رنگ و بوی عبیر
ز بالین دیبا سرش بر گرفت — چو بیدار شد تنگ در بر گرفت
نگه کرد برنا بدان خوب روی — بدان برز و بالا و آن روی و موی

31. *The Story of Haftvad and the Worm*

From Shah Tahmasp's BOOK OF KINGS, folio 521 verso
Signed: "Dust-Muhammad painted this."

Ca. 1540
406 x 267 mm. (miniature only)
Private Collection

Near an impoverished but hardworking village, the local girls met regularly on a hillside to spin. One day the daughter of Haftvad bit into an apple and discovered a worm. Sparing it, she exclaimed to her friends: "I am now the worm's lucky star. Just watch me outspin all of you today!" Her boast was justified; by the end of the day she had spun twice as much as usual. The girl spun such prodigious amounts that her father, Haftvad, abandoned all other work and focused his total attention on nurturing the worm. Haftvad and his town grew prosperous, while the worm became fat and sleek. Eventually Haftvad constructed a fortress with a special tank for the giant creature.

When Shah Ardashir learned about the worm, he considered its power a threat and set out to destroy it. After a preliminary defeat at the hands of Haftvad's army, Ardashir devised a clever scheme. Disguised as a merchant he would visit Haftvad and claim that he had so benefited from the worm's magic that he wished to receive its blessing. Haftvad fell victim to the deceit and a group of Ardashir's men gained entry into the worm's bastion. While the conspirators entertained the guards with food and wine, Ardashir fed the elephant-sized worm another kind of beverage—a potful of boiling lead. The death throes of the worm shook the whole fortress. Yet, before Haftvad could rally his troops, Ardashir's forces had stormed the stronghold and seized the town. Haftvad and his seven sons were hung and slain with a shower of arrows. S. R. C.

Dust-Muhammad—whom we have met already as the author of the Preface to the album he assembled for Shah Tahmasp in 1544/45, with its invaluable eye-witness accounts of his fellow artists—was a pupil of Bizhad. Possibly he went with his master from Herat to Tabriz in the company of Prince Tahmasp in 1522; or possibly he joined them slightly later. He worked on the Leningrad *Ball and Mallet* of 1524/25 (fig. 8), and painted several miniatures for the *Shahnama* project (see no. 34). Perhaps as long as a decade later, at the same time that no. 27 was inserted, Dust-Muhammad added this ambitiously large picture to the already completed volume.[1] Although his work is not found in Shah Tahmasp's *Quintet*, other signed miniatures and calligraphic specimens by him are in the Bahram Mirza Album.

Hardly the outstanding artist of his generation, he was nonetheless one of its most intriguing minds; and his career could be the basis for a peripatetic novel. The strange distortion of figures and trees, the saggingly diagonal composition, and the disturbing rock spirits of *Haftvad and the Worm* offer true insight into Dust-Muhammad's multi-faceted and unusual personality. Clearly proud of this painting, Dust-Muhammad designed it to illustrate several incidents simultaneously. Our interest, however, is caught by such personalities as the graybeards on the roof, with their elongated, mannered faces, and their hands

صورة ٥ دوست محمد

with the over-large, almost jointless thumbs characteristic of Dust-Muhammad's figures throughout his career. Like all of them, these peer blankly into space, further contributing to the "Gothic" mood. It is hardly surprising that Dust-Muhammad signed his poetry as *Mahi*, which means "The Waner" or "The Straw-man." Nor is it surprising that a contemporary Mughal source, Bayazid, tells us that Dust-Muhammad, although uninvited by Emperor Humayun, left Safavid Iran for the Mughal court because "he could not get by without the wine the Shah had forbidden." Bayazid also noted that Dust-Muhammad left on his own, unannounced, at the same time that a party of invited scholars and artists—notably Mir Sayyid-'Ali and 'Abd us-Samad—joined the emperor at Kabul on the first of November, 1549. He described Mulla Dust, as he called him, as "the top painter of them all," and said that he took up service with Prince Kamran, the rival and brother of Humayun in Afghanistan.[2]

OPPOSITE PAGE: Detail of no. 31.

1. For color reproductions, see Welch, *A King's Book of Kings*, pp. 173, 174.

2. For a portrait of Humayun and his court of this period attributable to Dūst-Muhammad, see Dickson and Welch, *The Houghton Shahnameh*, fig. 169. The portrait is in the so-called Jahangir Album, now in the Berlin State Library. The same album contains an early seventeenth-century Mughal version of *Haftvad and the Worm*, presumably based upon a drawing or tracing of the original brought to the Mughal court by the artist.

نوشتیم جان ورا آفرین — که از بدسگالان نشست او برین

چو شاپور شاپور گردد بلند — شود نزد او تاج و گاه ارجمند

سپارم بدو تاج و گنج و سپاه — که پیمان چنین بست شاپور شاه

من این تخت را پایکار رویم — همان از پدر یادگار رویم

شما یکسره داد یاد آورید — بکوشید و آیین داد آورید

چنان دان که خوردیم و بر ما گذشت — چو رفتی همه رنج ما باد گشت

چو رفتی همه دل بیزدان نهیم — روان را بدانجا گروگان نهیم

چو ده سال گیتی همی داشت راست — بخورد و ببخشید از انسان که خواست

نجست از کسی باج و ساو و خراج — همی ایکان داشت آن تخت عاج

مر او را نکوکار زان خواندند — که هر کس تن آسان ازو ماندند

چو شاپور گشت از در تاج و گاه — مر او را سپردان همه گنج شاه

نخست آن دلاور به پیمان خویش — ببردی که داشت سامان خویش

32. *The Accession of Ardashir II*

From Shah Tahmasp's BOOK OF KINGS, folio 547 recto
Probably by 'Abd ul-'Aziz, supervised by Aqa-Mirak

Ca. 1530–35
205 x 169 mm. (miniature only)
Lent by Arthur A. Houghton, Jr.

On the death of Shapur II, Ardashir II ascended the throne and summoned the notables of the realm to an audience with him. The Shah addressed the Iranians as follows: "It is our sincere desire that in our time the coursing heavens will bring no man to grief . . . Now, our late brother entrusted the realm to us specifically because his own son is still so young. (God rest the soul of one who purged the world of its malcontents!) When Shapur, son of Shapur [ultimately Shapur III] is of age to understand the meaning of throne and crown, we shall—as covenanted with his late majesty—surrender to him the state treasury and the military forces of the land. We act as caretaker to young Shapur's throne, and serve him as a living reminder of his father . . ."

Known as "Ardashir the Good," the Shah ruled with justice and without taxation for ten years. When Shapur III came of age, Ardashir II kept his word and transferred all the state treasury to his successor. S. R. C.

In the later years of the *Shahnama* project, when there were wider gaps between illustrations, new combinations of talent worked in up-to-date idioms. At first, this throne scene seems unfamiliar in style; but close study discloses tell tale habits of hand that we associate with 'Abd ul-'Aziz: his serpentine wiggles, slightly calmed, still permeate figures and flowers; and his unparalleled facial types, though painted more suavely, are still recognizable. Aqa-Mirak's influence is also apparent here, although we find no traces of his brushwork, in the overall cleanness of workmanship, in the "spotting" of the composition, poses stopped in mid-action, and in such minor details as turban types.

بزد تیر بر پشت آن گور نر / گذر کرد بر گور پیکان و پر

نر و ماده را هر دو بر هم بدوخت / دل لشکر از زخم او بر فروخت

ز لشکر هر آنکس که آن زخم دید / بر آن شاخ و یال آفرین گسترید / که چشم بد از فر تو دور باد / همه روزگاران تو سور باد

بمردی تو اندر زمانه نوی / که هم شاه و هم پهلوان گوی / وز انجا بر انگیخت شبرنگ شاه / یکی بیشه پیش اندر آمد براه

دو شیر ژیان پیش آن بیشه دید / کمان را بزه کرد و اندر کشید / بزد بر بر و سینهٔ شیر چاک / گذر کرد تا پر و پیکان بخاک

بر ماده شد تیز و بگشاد شست / بر شیر با کرد رانش بخست / سپاهش همه خواندند آفرین / که ای نامور شهریار زمین

ندید و نه بشنید کس اندر جهان / چو تو شاه بر گاه شاهنشهان / که با تیر نی پر تو شیر افکنی / پی کوه خارا زبن بر کنی

33. *Bahram Gur Pins the Coupling Onagers*

From Shah Tahmasp's BOOK OF KINGS, folio 568 recto
Attributable to Mir Sayyid-'Ali

Ca. 1533–35
207 x 172 mm. (miniature only)
Lent by The Metropolitan Museum of Art, Gift of Arthur A. Houghton, Jr., 1970 (1970.301.62)

Hunting on a spring day with a thousand horsemen, the Sasanian Shah, Bahram, and his minister, Ruzbih, happened upon a plain overrun with wild asses, who had gathered to spar and mate. Bahram readied his bow and arrow as he watched two bucks butt and scrape. When the victor mounted a jennet, Bahram let fly his arrow and pinned the two animals together. This episode earned the Shah the nickname Bahram Gur or "Onagers" Bahram. S. R. C.

More original and accomplished than Mir Sayyid-'Ali's *Rustam and the "Seven" Champions Hunting in Turan* (no. 20), this miniature dates from his early maturity and is his latest single-handed picture for the project. Proud of the accomplishment, he enhanced the page with unique ornamental flourishes of arabesque between the columns of text and surrounding the calligraphy. By now, the artist's painstakingly fine workmanship was being applied to his own pictures as well as to those he helped finish for the senior masters. Bahram Gur's turban and saddlecloth look forward promisingly to similarly detailed passages in his pictures for the *Quintet* (nos. 61, 66–68). Especially characteristic are the colorful simurgh on the saddlecloth, a motif the artist painted with particular flair, and the accurate articulation of the quiver, bow, and arrows.[1]

Stylistically, this miniature seems of about the same date as *A Princely Procession*, also attributable to Mir Sayyid-'Ali, in a copy of Jami's *Yusuf and Zulaykha*, dated 1533/34, now in the National Library, Cairo.[2]

1. For color reproductions, see Welch, *A King's Book of Kings*, pp. 176, 177.

2. See Stchoukine, *Les Peintures des manuscrits safavis de 1502 à 1587*, pl. 16.

34. *Nushirvan Greets the Khaqan's Daughter*

From Shah Tahmasp's BOOK OF KINGS, folio 633 verso
Attributable to Dust-Muhammad

Ca. 1530
185 x 180 mm. (miniature only)
Lent by The Metropolitan Museum of Art, Gift of Arthur A. Houghton, Jr., 1970 (1970.301.70)

The Khaqan of Chin and his army had conquered all of Transoxiana and were poised to invade Iran when the Khaqan's magi advised him to sue for peace instead. An envoy journeyed to the Sasanian Shah Nushirvan's camp with the peace proposal. Following the Shah's acceptance of the bid, the Khaqan dispatched a second embassy offering a Turanian princess in marriage to the Shah in order to cement the agreement. The Shah's representative journeyed to the Turkish camp where he was given his choice of five princesses. He selected the only daughter of the Khaqan by his royal wife and queen, the others being daughters of concubines. Back across Turan along the highroad into Iran the splendid bridal caravan wended its way. In Gurgan myriad perfumes wafted through the air and trumpets blared out in anticipation of the arrival of Nushirvan's bride. When at last her cavalcade reached the royal residence, the Shah was overcome by the beauty of her moon-like face and her scented, braided hair. Nushirvan whispered thanks to God again and again for this lovely new jewel in his crown. S. R. C.

Dust-Muhammad's pictures for the *Shahnama* project, as compared to his added "masterpiece," *Haftvad and the Worm*, are less ambitious and accomplished, clearly earlier and less consequential. They are, however, stylistic precursors to it and identical in style to signed works in the Bahram Mirza Album. Although the present miniature is outstanding in the series, the figures, with their "gracefully" arcing silhouettes, seem weak in the knees or jointless—a mannerism he passed on to his apprentice, Shaykh-Muhammad (see fig. 9). Other identifying quirks are also evident—ill-fitting turbans, atop faces that often appear disturbingly flat and hesitant, almost tremulous outline drawing. But Dust-Muhammad's strengths are also apparent, in the illusive gentleness of characterizations, in his muted, very personal colors, and in the superbly designed and executed calligraphic inscriptions.

Inscribed

over portico at upper left, eighth couplet of Hafiz' Ode No. 179
Above this chrysolite arch they have inscribed so in gold:
"Apart from the good of the pure in heart—nothing endures."

همه بار ایشان ز مشک و می / شکر با درم ریخته زیر پی
چو آمد بت اندر شبستان شاه / بهمد اندرون کرد کسری نگاه
زبس ناله نای و چنگ و رباب / نبد بر زمین جای آرام و خواب

کلاهی بکردار مشکین زره / طبق کشیده گره در گره
گره بسته از ناز و برتافته / بافسون یک اندر دگر بافته
یکی سرو دید از برش گرد ماه / نهاده بمه بر ز عنبر کلاه

چو بر غالیه بر گل انگشتری
همه زیر انگشتری مشتری

بدو شاد نوشین روان خیره ماند / بر و نام یزدان فراوان بخواند
شهر او را جایی بگزید شاه / بیاراستند از بر گاه ماه
چو آگاهی آمد بخاقان چین / ز ایران و از شاه ایران زمین
وز آن شادمانی بفرزند او / شدند شاد و خرم به پیوند او
بپرداخت هر شهر قند و حاج / بقیجعا رباشتی فرستاد و تاج
از این شهرها چون رفت آگاه / همه مرزبانان فرستاد شاه
جهان شد پر از داد نوشین روان / ببخشند بر پشت پیر و جوان
بیکایک همی خواندند آفرین / بهر جایی بر شاه ایران زمین
همه دست برداشته باسمان / که ای کردگار مکان و زمان
توانی و دیگر شاه کسری مدار / بگردان ز جانش بد روزگار

35. Nushirvan Responds to the Questions of the Grand Magus

From Shah Tahmasp's BOOK OF KINGS, folio 655 verso
Attributable to Mir Musavvir, assisted by Qasim Son of 'Ali (?)

Ca. 1530–35
231 x 173 mm. (miniature only)
Lent by Arthur A. Houghton, Jr.

The Grand Magus asked Nushirvan the following question: "We see two men praying with equal faith and fervor for something each craves. The one gets his wish and is blessed with joy; the other receives nothing but tears for his face and furrows for his brow. How is it that God hears the prayers of one but not of another?" The Shah replied: "The mercy a man craves of God must be within measure. A desire for excess can only earn one a broken heart." The magus posed another question: "What man is properly called good and deserving of the name 'great'?" Nushirvan responded, "Certainly not a ruler who leaves the treasury wasted. Such a man, in effect, is wasting his time. For, sooner or later, his fortune will turn against him. To be called 'great' you must be known for your fortune, famed for your generosity; to be good, you cannot hold unstintingly to all you possess." In a similar fashion the magus proceeded with thirty-odd questions for which the Shah provided reasoned, ethical responses. S.R.C.

Chronologically and stylistically comparable to *The Accession of Ardashir II* (no. 32), this painting is by a different pair of artists. Mir Musavvir's restrained caricature of court attendants, often shown in open-mouthed profile, his rounded rock forms, resembling potatoes, and his harmoniously curving outlines attest to his close involvement, whereas many less authoritative passages, such as the face in the upper right and the somewhat insensitively regularized flowers and grass-tufts, bear all the earmarks of his usual assistant (see also nos. 21, 37).

چنین گوید از دفتر پهلوان　　که پرسید موبد ز نوشیروان

که آن چیست گر گردکار جهان　　بخواهد پرستنده اندر نهان

بدان آرزو نیز پاسخ دهد　　بپاسخ ورا بخت فرخ نهد

یکی دست برداشته باسپمان　　همی خواهد از کردگار جهان

بموبد چنین گفت پیروز شاه　　فزونی ز یزدان باندازه خواه

بپرسید نیکی کرا درخورست　　بنام بزرگی که زیباترست

ببخشش نباشد سزاوار تخت　　زمان تا زمان تیره گردد ز بخت

نیابد بخواهش همی آرزوی　　دو چشمش پر از آب و پر چین بروی

جو خواهش از اندازه افزون شود　　از آن آرزو دل پر از خون شود

چنین داد پاسخ که هر کس که گنج　　پراکنده یابد بنا برده رنج

36. *Khusraw Parviz Braves the Three Turks at the Nahravan*

From Shah Tahmasp's BOOK OF KINGS, folio 690 verso
Attributable to Aqa-Mirak

Ca. 1530–35
304 x 261 mm. (miniature only)
Lent by Arthur A. Houghton, Jr.

The Sasanian Shah Khusraw-Parviz gathered his armies near the Nahravan Canal to quell the rebel Bahram Chubina. Unfortunately for the Shah, Bahram Chubina's agents had infiltrated the royal camp so totally that the enemy was apprised of the Shah's most secret strategies. Upon learning that his troops had swung their allegiance to Bahram Chubina, Khusraw and his closest advisers withdrew from the army to observe from nearby heights the happenings of the night. Soon the inevitable attack began, led by three bloodthirsty Turks. Khusraw watched the slaughter of his men, distraught and grieving until he could stand the sight no more. He then plunged into the fray and took on all three Turks. As one of the Turks charged, Khusraw thrust his sword and felled him. Despite this triumph the Shah's troops abandoned him. His only alternative was to flee the battlefield and return to his palace at Ctesiphon. With Bahram Chubina nearing the capital, Khusraw escaped, slipping across the Euphrates into Rum. S. R. C.

One of the challenges braved by Aqa-Mirak was carrying out his extensive series of boldly simplified compositions for the vast *Shahnama*, a task that few artists could have completed without resorting to dreary formulae, or allowing sloppy workmanship. If self-discipline contributed to their success, so did the fact that each miniature posed new compositional problems, the solution to which can be compared to a musician scoring variations on a theme. Here we share the artist's pleasure in the placement of the two shields of Khusraw-Parviz and his tumbling opponent. Like two nailheads, they sustain a design that would otherwise fall flat. But this brightly ornamental painting depends upon perfectly positioned accents: the sinuous form of the rivulet above the hero echoes and reinforces his horse's lunge; and the bitingly sharp diagonals of spears and swordblades establish an exciting counterpoint. As usual in this series, the impassivity of the warriors is foiled by the grotesques in the rocks, in this case particularly by a camel's head, far left, protesting the trumpet's blare.

بگردنکشان گفت یاری کنید — برین نامور کامگاری کنید
بباید دمان تا بر آن سه ترک — نه ترک دلاور سه شیر سترگ
همیخواست زد بر سر شهریار — سپر در سر آورد شاه سوار
بزیر سپر تیغ زهرابگون — بزد تیغ و انداختش سرنگون
که پرویز گر پشت و یار منست — همان گرز و شمشیر کار منست
یکی تاخت تا پیش خسرو رسید — برند آوری از میان برکشید

ببندوی و گستهم گفت آن زمان — که اکنون شدم زین سخن بدگمان
اگر من شوم کشته در کارزار — جهان را نباشد یکی شهریار
خروشید کای نامداران جنگ — زمانی دگر گرد باید درنگ
سپاهش همه روی برگاشتند — جهانجوی را خوار بگذاشتند
رسیده مرا هیچ فرزند نیست — همان از در تاج و پیوند نیست
بدو گفت بندوی کای سرفراز — جهان را به مهر تو بادا نیاز

37. *Bahram Chubina Slays Kappi the Lion-Ape*

From Shah Tahmasp's BOOK OF KINGS, folio 715 verso
By Mir Musavvir, assisted by Qasim Son of 'Ali (?)

Ca. 1535
214 x 188 mm. (miniature only)
Lent by The Metropolitan Museum of Art, Gift of Arthur A. Houghton, Jr., 1970 (1970.301.74)

Defeated at the hands of Khusraw-Parviz, Bahram Chubina fled to the lands of Turk and Chin, where he resolved in gratitude to rid the Khaqan's realm of an overly powerful paladin and a fierce lion-ape. After making short work of the paladin, Bahram turned to the lion-ape, Kappi, who lived in a grove where he had devoured the Khaqan's daughter. On Bahram's approach, Kappi submerged himself in a spring. Gnashing teeth and breathing fire, Kappi sprang from the water and tried to suck Bahram into his fiendish jaws. With arrow and mace blows Bahram slew the beast, hacked it in two, and tossed aside its severed head.

The Khaqan and his subjects rejoiced at the news of Bahram's success, which, however, alarmed the Iranian Shah, Khusraw-Parviz. After infiltrating the Khaqan's palace, one of the Shah's agents found Bahram and stabbed him to death. S.R.C.

Mir Musavvir ended his sequence of miniatures with a dying monster which he transformed into a beguiling delight. As interpreted by the Mir, the rosy-rumped, polka-dotted lion-ape seems far less deserving of slaughter than the dour and squat Bahram Chubina. It may even be that Mir Musavvir sided with Kappi (whom he himself painted) against his killer (who was left to the mercy of his assistant). Also worthy of attention are Mir Musavvir's earth-spirits which turn away in horror, glower disapprovingly, or giggle smugly. One wonders if anyone, including Shah Tahmasp, ever devoted sufficient time to the enjoyment of such passages.

OPPOSITE PAGE: Detail of no. 37.
Complete miniature at right.

زننده بدان سرو بر داشت رود
سرودی باواز خوش بر کشید
بدان نامداران بفرمود شاه
جهاندیده آگاهی اندر گرفت
بیاورد جامی دگر
زننده دگرگونه آراست رود
همان ساخته
که اکنون بخوانیش داد آفرید
که از بخت شاه این نباشد شگفت
چو از خوب رخ بستد آن شهریار
بر آورد ناگاه بانگ سرود
یکی نغز دستان بزد بر درخت
بماندند یکسر همه در شگفت
فراوان بجستند و باز آمدند
که گردد گل و سرو رامشگرش
گران خیره شد مردم شادبخت
همی هر کسی رای دیگر گرفت
بنزدیک خسرو فراز آمدند
که جاوید بادا بر و افسرش
که بیکار گردش همی خواندند
بفرمود کین را بجای آورید
چنین نام از آواز او راندند
همه باغ یکسر بپای آورید
جوان داناش گفت و خسرو شنید
بجستند بسیار هر سوی باغ
باواز او جام می در کشید
ببردند زیر درختان چراغ

38. *Barbad the Concealed Musician*

From Shah Tahmasp's BOOK OF KINGS, folio 731 recto
Attributable to Mirza-'Ali

Ca. 1535
316 x 268 mm. (miniature only)
Lent by Arthur A. Houghton, Jr.

The glorious court of Khusraw-Parviz encouraged a flowering of the arts; and musicians such as the royal favorite Sarkash, enjoyed high standing. Thus, when the minstrel Barbad, an "unknown," sought recognition at court, Sarkash, fearing his eclipse by this brilliant rival, bribed the royal chamberlain to keep Barbad out of Khusraw's presence. Bent on playing for the Shah, Barbad befriended the royal gardener who tended the private garden in which the Shah celebrated Nowruz. He allowed Barbad to climb a cypress tree from which he overlooked Khusraw's dais.

As evening set in Barbad began to play his lute. Khusraw and his courtiers listened, absorbed in the lovely strains issuing from the hidden lute. Each song delighted the Shah more than the last. Although he ordered a search, the minstrel could not be found. Finally, when Khusraw exclaimed that he would stuff the musician's mouth with pearls and precious stones if he were discovered, Barbad tumbled out of the tree and prostrated himself at Khusraw's feet. Upon hearing Barbad's tale, Khusraw appointed him court musician and banished the evil Sarkash. S. R. C.

Eager to please, the youthful Mirza-'Ali packed every inch of this miniature with his personal interpretations of Safavid pictorial clichés: richly dressed courtiers (fat as pouter pigeons as in all his youthful work); orientalized dragonish clouds (with the Mirza's added smokiness); and tapestry-like verdure (designed by him in pinwheeled clusters). Touches of naturalism abound, as in the cook, foreground, fanning the flames with his skirt. Like the rest of the picture, rocks and cliffs are in Mirza-'Ali's early style, spongy—with a cast of pleasant, smiling ghouls.[1]

1. For a color reproduction, see Welch, *Persian Painting*, pl. 10.

39. The Assassination of Khusraw Parviz

From Shah Tahmasp's BOOK OF KINGS, folio 742 verso
Attributable to 'Abd us-Samad

Ca. 1535
271 x 257 mm. (miniature only)
Lent by The Metropolitan Museum of Art, Gift of Arthur A. Houghton, Jr., 1970 (1970.301.75)

Iran waged war against the Qaysar for twenty-five years, after which Khusraw's injustices alienated his subjects. To restore the crown to glory, the Shah's confidant and an important general plotted his overthrow. After one of their agents had freed Prince Shiruya from prison, the conspirators hired an assassin—a filthy-footed, foul-smelling vagrant named Mihr-Hurmuzd. When the assassin entered Khusraw's antechamber, the terrified Shah sent his page for water, a golden ewer, and fresh garments in the hope that the boy would bring help. But the naive youth returned alone. Mihr Hurmuzd bolted the door and stabbed the praying Shah to death. S. R. C.

'Abd us-Samad's career at the Safavid court lasted only until he joined the Mughals in 1549 and is largely undocumented in Safavid sources. The Mughal historian Abu'l Fazl says the artist was from Shiraz; we suspect he came to the royal workshop in the early 1530s. The present picture we attribute to him by comparison with signed works.[1] Painted shortly before the end of the Shahnama project, it probably marks his acceptance as a young master in the Shah's atelier, and is his only work in the manuscript. Neatly if not innovatively designed, it contains figures 'Abd us-Samad employed elsewhere—the bald-headed sleeping man and the slightly rodent-like youths.[2] None of his work appears in the Shah's *Quintet*, and according to Abu'l Fazl he sought service with the Mughal emperor Humayun during his Tabriz visit. Summoned to the Mughal court with Mir Sayyid 'Ali in 1546, he and his companions reached Kabul in 1549 and in 1554 departed with Humayun for India. There he underwent a crucial change of style under Humayun's son Akbar's patronage and, says Abu'l Fazl, "he was stirred to new heights by the alchemy of Akbar's vision, and he turned from outer forms to inner meaning." Successful as a courtier and government official, he held a number of significant posts. As an artist, he was far more important in India than in Iran, and can be considered with Mir Sayyid-'Ali as co-founder of the Mughal school.

1. For color reproductions, see Welch, *A King's Book of Kings*, pp. 185, 187.

2. See Laurence Binyon, J. V. S. Wilkinson, and Basil Gray, *Persian Miniature Painting* (London: Oxford University Press, 1933) pls. 104 and 105. Also see Dickson and Welch, *The Houghton Shahnameh*, figs. 250, 252.

ز پیشش بیامد پرستار چند
چو برسم بدید اندر آمد بباز
یکی چادر نو بسر در کشید
سبک باز شد جامه زو در کشید
جگرگاه شاه جهان بر درید
یکی طشت زرین بر شاه برد
نه گاه سخن بود و هنگام راز
بدان تا رخ جان ستان پا زبد
ابا جامه و با پرستار آب
همی جامه ها را بپوشید شاه
بشد مهر هرمز ز خنجر ببست
همی کرد خسرو بر دین شتاب
به زمزم همی توبه کرد از گناه
در خانه با پادشا را ببست
سخن سنج بی رنج اگر مرد لاف
بی آزاری و راستی برگزین
همان بدگمانان بزندان شدند
بزندان بکشتندشان بیگناه
ببینید ز کردار او جز گزاف
چو خواهی که یابی بداد آفرین
بایوان آن مستمندان شدند
بدانگه که برگشته بد بخت شاه
اگر گنج یابی اگر درد و رنج
چو آگاهی آمد ببازار و راه
گرامی ده و پنج فرزند بود
جهاندار چیزی نیارست گفت
برین گونه گردد جهان تا جهان
همی راز خویش از تو دارد نهان
نمانی همی در سرای سپنج
که خسرو بر آن گونه بر شد تباه
بایوان شاهی که پابند بود
همیداشت آن انده اندر نهفت

Divan of Hafiz

This manuscript of the *Divan* ("Collected Works") of Shams ud-Din Muhammad Hafiz (born ca. 1326, died 1390) was copied and illustrated for—or given to—Shah Tahmasp's brother, Sam Mirza, whose name appears on folio 86 recto, *The Celebration of 'Id* (no. 43). There is no colophon; scribe unknown; and the manuscript is not dated. But the style of the miniatures argues for a date of ca. 1526/27, on the basis of close links to the Paris Nava'i (Bibliothèque Nationale supp. turc 316, 317). There were once five miniatures, one of which is lost (see Stuart Cary Welch, *Persian Painting: Five Royal Safavid Manuscripts of the Sixteenth Century* (New York: Braziller, 1976) fig. C); for the others, including Sultan-Muhammad's only two signed works, and one signed by Shaykh-Zadeh, see below (nos. 42, 43, 44). The manuscript contains 176 folios and a double page *unvan* (no. 40). Folios measure 290 by 182 mm.

This manuscript was formerly in the collection of Louis J. Cartier and is now on deposit at the Fogg Art Museum, Harvard University.

OPPOSITE PAGE: Detail of no. 41.

40. Double Page Frontispiece

From the COLLECTED WORKS of Hafiz

Ca. 1526/27
290 x 182 mm. (each folio)
Private Collection

Just as the styles of painting during the late fifteenth and early sixteenth centuries differed between Eastern and Western Iran, so did the styles of ornament. Western ornament, centered at Tabriz, was usually more dynamic rhythmically, and richer in color, even to the point of excess. Eastern, centered at Herat, tended to be more restrained, with subtler rhythms and color harmonies, and often was finer in scale. This frontispiece, dating from a period of fusion between Eastern and Western elements, nonetheless retains an Eastern flavor—presumably because its artist was trained at Herat, if indeed the manuscript itself was not made there.

41. Royal Lovers Picnicking in a Garden

From the COLLECTED WORKS of Hafiz, folio 67 verso
Attributable to Sultan-Muhammad

Ca. 1526/27
190 x 124 mm. (miniature only)
Private Collection

Hafiz' lines inscribed at the top of this miniature evoke romance—

> *"A rose without the glow of a lover bears no joy;*
> *Without wine to drink the spring brings no joy."*[1]

Idealized, moon-faced young lovers, a *saqi* (page boy) offering wine, dancing girls, and musicians, all set within a flowery garden at dusk—an Iranian's heaven-on-earth. The ensemble borders on sentimental triteness yet avoids it. For the lovers' faces are genuinely tender; their canopy, with its stunning, lashing arabesques, evokes raw passion; and the oranges and blues of robe and coat, hardly soothing, burn and freeze our eyes. Like love itself, the effect of the painting is wondrous, ecstasy's sweet sting!

Unlike Sultan-Muhammad's two other miniatures for this manuscript, this one is unsigned—perhaps because there was no convenient place to inscribe. The style, however, is of a piece with the others, which, as his only signed works, are the touchstones of his artistic personality. All three miniatures conform to the style of *The Court of Gayumars* (no. 8), which was still in progress at this date, and likewise shows the impact of Bihzad's finesse and psychological concern on Sultan-Muhammad's earlier, visionary manner. The radiant prince here, with his rounded lap and wave-like skirt edges, might be a youthful portrayal of Gayumars himself, while the "Chinese" trees, with their nervous curves, seem small-scaled versions of those growing near his mountainous throne.[2]

1. The new translations for the Hafiz miniatures are by Martin Bernard Dickson.

2. For color reproductions, see Basil Gray, *Persian Painting* (Lausanne: Skira, 1961) p. 137; and Welch, *Persian Painting*, p. 117.

کل بی رخ یار خوش نباشد
بی باده بهار خوش نباشد

واعظان کین جلوه در محراب و منبر میکنند
چون بخلوت میروند آن کار دیگر میکنند

42. *Episode in a Mosque*

From the COLLECTED WORKS of Hafiz, folio 77 recto
Inscribed: "done by Shaykh-Zadeh"

Ca. 1536/37
250 x 144 mm. (miniature only)
Private Collection

Professor Martin Bernard Dickson's delightful translations of the lines from Hafiz inscribed on this painting are as follows:

in upper left corner
Preachers preening on the pulpit praying loudly for us all,
Take their vows and on the quiet answer to a different call.[1]
over the main portico
Mind your own business, preacher man, what are you yowling for?
I've lost my heart in love and you—what are you prowling for?[2]
on balustrade of roof on far left
There's a ready site where you may nest in the recess of my eyes.[3]

The mid 1520s were crucial years in the formation of the Safavid style, the moment when Eastern and Western ideologies met and merged. In the royal workshop it must have been a time of strain and tension and such moods are reflected in the miniatures. Even mighty Sultan-Muhammad, whose artistic powers can be likened to a great river forced by a change of terrain to alter its course, can be seen from his pictures to have been shaken. But these critical years seem to have been yet harder for Shaykh-Zadeh, whose masterpiece this is. For he not only had been trained at Herat under Bihzad, but due to the latter's virtual retirement from active painting upon moving to Tabriz (because of failing eyesight?), he became the leading practitioner of Bihzad's art. Many Bihzadian pictures attributable on stylistic grounds to him and to his apprentices, among whom we include Mirza-'Ali, are found in the Metropolitan Museum of Art's *Khamsa* of Nizami[4] of 1524/25 and the Paris Nava'i of 1526/27. In the present picture, however, he seems to have been put on his mettle, and to have verged from the Herat idiom. Although the ravishing intricacy and variety of ornament proclaim his creative determination and desire to please the patron, they conform to the tradition of Herat. The figures, however, were interpreted with urgency and drama unprecedented in his illustrations to the Nizami and Nava'i, qualities associated with Sultan-Muhammad. Significantly, Shaykh-Zadeh, who had been so influential and active in the Safavid school of the mid 1520s did not contribute either to the *Shahnama* (in which his influence is apparent, as in no. 7) or to the *Quintet*. His future lay at the Uzbek court of Bukhara, where he became the primary artistic force.[5, 6]

1. In *nasta'liq*, the opening couplet of Hafiz' Ode No. 199. See: Hafiz, *Dīvān-i Khwājeh Shams ud-Dīn Muhammad Hāfiẓ-i Shīrāẓī*, Muhammad Qazvīnī and Qāsim Ghani, eds. (Tehrān: Kitābkhāneh-y Zavvār, 1320/1941)

2. In *naskh*, the opening couplet of Hafiz' Ode No. 35. See: Hafiz, *Dīvān*.

3. In *naskh*, first half of opening couplet of Hafiz' Ode No. 34. See: Hafiz, *Dīvān*.

4. See Peter J. Chelkowski, and Priscilla P. Soucek, *Mirror of the Invisible World. Tales from the Khamseh of Niẓami* (New York: The Metropolitan Museum of Art, 1975).

5. For a signed double-page miniature in a *Haft Manẓar* of Hatifi, copied at Bukhara for Sultan 'Abd ul-'Aziz in 1537; see Dickson and Welch, The *Houghton Shahnameh*, figs. 41 and 42.

6. For a color reproduction, see Welch, *Persian Painting*, pl. 16.

43. *The Celebration of 'Id*

From the COLLECTED WORKS of Hafiz, folio 86 recto
Inscribed: "done by Sultan-Muhammad of 'Iraq"[1]

Ca. 1526/27
248 x 147 mm. (miniature only)
Private Collector

Hafiz's Ode describes the feast, ending the fast of Ramadan, which begins with the sighting of the new moon. We quote the couplets inscribed along the balustrade of the roof:

It's the 'Id and a time for roses—and a goodly company await.
Saqi: See the moon in the face of the Shah—and bring the wine.
How grandiose his future, how benignly grand a King!
God grant his time immunity from the blight of the evil-eye!

Although the name of Shah Tahmasp's brother Sam Mirza is written over the doorway, Martin Bernard Dickson has pointed out that the accompanying titles are the Shah's. Inasmuch as the inscription, unlike the immaculately designed signature on the throne, seems to have been tampered with, the manuscript probably was presented by the Shah, for whom it was made, to Prince Sam. The choice of the Ode, with its allusion to a king, further supports this belief. For whichever patron it was painted, this miniature is vital to the understanding of Sultan-Muhammad. His favorite compositional device, here a flickering oval of white turbans, brings to mind the flame-like arrangement of courtiers in the *Court of Gayumars*, in the left foreground of which we find one of the artist's recurring personalities—a handsome Caucasian, shown in profile, who also occupies the center foreground of this signed miniature. The artist's penchant for sharply witty anecdote is exemplified by the row of moon-watchers atop the pavilion, whose attitudes vary from grimly serious piety to utter boredom, hypocrisy, and devil-may-care amorousness. Side glances and cunningly observed gestures churn ripples of fun and innuendo through the picture.[2]

Inscribed

over doorway
The Fighter for the Faith, Abu'l Muzaffar [The Ever-victorious] *Prince Sam*

1. 'Iraq—i.e., Western Iran

2. For color reproductions, see Arthur Upham Pope, ed., *Survey of Persian Art from Prehistoric Times to the Present*, 6 vols. (Oxford: Oxford University Press, 1939–1958) pl. 900. Also see Welch, *Persian Painting*, pl. 17.

گرفته ساغر عشرت فرشته رحمت
ز جرعه بر رخ حور و پری گلاب زده

44. *Allegory of Drunkenness*

From the COLLECTED WORKS of Hafiz, folio 135 recto
Signed: Sultan-Muhammad

Ca. 1526/27
215 x 150 mm. (miniature only)
Private Collection

An exploration of worldly and other-worldly drunkenness, this miniature, like Hafiz's poetry, is both profoundly serious and mordantly comical.[1] A portrayal of Hafiz himself, pop-eyed with drink, in an upper window, sets the mood. To his right, in another window, an evil worldling tempts an innocent and worried child with his first quaff of wine, while below a tipsy reveler lurches testily through the tavern door. His swollen head and dizzily shaped body, recalling *Rustam Asleep* (no. 2), exemplify Sultan-Muhammad's genius for conveying sensation by transforming what he had seen or imagined into abstraction. At the left, three fur-clad *qalandars*, the most extreme of Sufi mystics, scream and bang, animal-men who amuse and unsettle us. Like the earth spirits surrounding Gayumars, they are grotesque and at the same time provide visual delight. In painting his human, sub-human and supra-human comedies, Sultan-Muhammad, the Sufi story-teller, was one with the artist. Unlike his followers, such as Qadimi, whose style was based on this phase of Sultan-Muhammad's work, he could integrate all facets of his personality, from the sublime to the outrageous.

Inscribed

at top, lines from an Ode of Hafiz

The angel of mercy took the reveling cup and tossed it down,
As rose-water, on the cheeks of houris and angels

1. For color reproductions, see Binyon, Wilkinson and Gray, *Persian Miniature Painting*, pl. LXXV. Also, see Welch, *Persian Painting*, pl. 18; and Basil W. Robinson, *Persian Drawings from the 14th through the 19th Century* (Boston and Toronto: Little, Brown and Co., 1965) pl. 34.

45. *Leopards and Bears in a Wood*

From a ROSE GARDEN of Sa'di
Border drawing attributable to Sultan-Muhammad

Ca. 1525–30
301 x 189 mm. (folio size); 150 x 87 mm. (text area)
Lent by the Museum of Fine Arts, Boston, Francis Bartlett Donation of 1912 and Picture Fund (14.608)

46. *A Fantastic Forest*

From a ROSE GARDEN of Sa'di
Border drawing attributable to Sultan-Muhammad

Ca. 1525–30
301 x 189 mm. (folio size); 150 x 87 mm. (text area)
Private Collection

Calligraphers, artists, illuminators, and paper-makers collaborated in Iran to create books as delightful to view and touch as to read. In this instance, a superbly calligraphed manuscript, with borders tinted in varied, marvelous hues, was further enriched by Shah Tahmasp's painters, who improvised border drawings in two tones of gold and silver. Many of its scattered folios were adorned by Sultan-Muhammad himself, with figures, angels, birds, and animals, including such fanciful ones as dragons, simurghs, and ch'i-lins. Stylistically, they are akin to many slightly earlier passages for the *Shahnama* (see color detail of flapping cranes, p. 6), and like them, they were influenced by the fifteenth-century Turkman designs that formed part of Shah Isma'il's booty at the fall of Tabriz in 1502. Sultan-Muhammad's spirited and dashing brushwork and inventive compositions, often with superbly interrelated diagonals are, however, markedly personal, and make this series of borders one of the most appealing in a long tradition.

According to F. R. Martin, the manuscript from which these borders were removed was acquired by the German art historian Phillipp Walter Schulz in Iran early in this century. Although a considerable literature has grown up about them, most of its facts are wrong.[1] The volume was misidentified as a *Bustan* of Sa'di rather than his *Gulistan*, and the superb calligraphy has been cited as by Sultan-'Ali of Mashhad, apparently on hearsay alone, as no one has recorded the existence a colophon. The fact remains, nonetheless, that these enchanting folios are among the highwater marks of Safavid book production, and their border drawings are even livelier than those of the later *Quintet* (see no. 52).[2]

1. For the literature on this so-called *Bustan*, see Robinson, et. al., *The Keir Collection*, pp. 181–182.

2. For a color reproduction of a page of text, see Laurence Binyon, *The Poems of Nizami* (London: Studio, 1928).

47. Inscribed: "*Sarkhan Bek the Steward*"[1]

Signed: "Mir Musavvir painted it."

Ca. 1530–40
321 x 308 mm. (miniature only)
By courtesy of the Trustees of the British Museum (1930.11.12.02)

Qazi Ahmad described Mir Musavvir as "a portraitist whose work was flawless. . . . who produced paintings of the utmost charm and elegance." On seeing this signed example, one fully agrees with the late sixteenth-century opinion. Although sadly, and literally, de-faced, the portly but graceful figure bears out the Qazi's words. His powerful, massive proportions combine happily, if incongruously, with delicately flower-like hands in a gracefully turning pose of astonishing lightness. It was on the basis of this signed picture that we first identified the Mir's miniatures for the *Shahnama*, such as *The Nightmare of Zuhhak* (no. 11), which contains stylistically identical personages.

Although Dust-Muhammad linked Mir Musavvir with Sultan-Muhammad and Aqa-Mirak as collaborators on the *Quintet* as well as the *Book of Kings*, his paintings for it are unknown, perhaps because they were separated when the volume was refurbished in the seventeenth century, or because they were never bound into it. Prior to the discovery of his miniatures for the *Shahnama*, the Mir was almost forgotten, despite his major reputation at Shah Tahmasp's court. Now, his major role as artist and teacher has become apparent. Artists of the second Safavid generation learned much from him. Mirza-'Ali's pictorial elegance, from the immaculate tailoring of his figures down to the graceful curves of finger-tips, follows the Mir's example; and if there are hints of tension between Mir Musavvir and his son, Mir Sayyid-'Ali, the latter's hyperaestheticism in abstracting the visible world into sinuous patterns, as well as his inventive concern for ornament stem from paternal example.

The artist's tendency to isolate a single area for intensively detailed finish is apparent in Sarkhan Bek's turban, which brings to mind Mir-Sayyid-'Ali's accuracy of observation and effective use of stripes. Despite the partial obliteration of the baton, it appears to be long and narrow, in the fashion of the later 1530s rather than earlier. Such hints are especially useful for dating Mir Musavvir's miniatures for due to his extreme subtlety, stylistic changes over the years are scarcely discernible.

1. Or, according to Norah Titley's new reading, *Mir Khan Beg Sufrachi* (the table-layer). See Norah M. Titley, *Miniatures from Persian Manuscripts: A Catalogue and Subject Index of Paintings from Persia, India, and Turkey in the British Library and the British Museum* (London: British Museum Publications, Ltd., 1977) p. 167, nos. 165, 395, for an earlier reading.

The Khamsa of Nizami

The *Khamsa* ("Quintet") written by Nizam ad-Din Ilyas ibn Yusuf called Nizami (born ca. 1140/41, died March 12, 1209) was copied by the renowned scribe Shah Mahmud of Nishapur "at Tabriz" from 1539–1543 A.D. for Shah Tahmasp, whose name appears on an architectural frieze in one of the miniatures (folio 60 verso, no. 57). Now in the collection of the British Library (Or. 2265), the *Quintet* contains 396 folios measuring 360 by 250 mm. Eleven of the fourteen contemporary miniatures remaining in the manuscript are inscribed, probably in the later hand of a well-informed librarian, with artists' names: Sultan-Muhammad, Aqa-Mirak, Mirza-'Ali, Mir Sayyid-'Ali, and Muzaffar-'Ali.

The manuscript was refurbished in the late seventeenth century, at which time many borders were replaced, several miniatures apparently were removed (see numbers 66 to 68), others were retouched, and three, not shown here, were added by Muhammad Zaman, who dated each of them A.H. 1086 (A.D. 1675).

48. Rosette

From Shah Tahmasp's QUINTET of Nizami, folio 1 verso

Ca. 1540
360 x 250 mm. (folio size)
Lent by the British Library (Or. 2265)

Unlike the opening rosette to the *Book of Kings* (no. 5), this superb passage of illumination does not contain the patron's titles and name. It also differs in style and mood from the earlier example, which seems more highly charged and vigorous, if less fine. Ornament, like painting, had become more restrained and elegant by the 1540s, closer to the classical style of late Timurid Herat than to the dynamic idiom of Turkman Tabriz.

49. Double Page Frontispiece

From Shah Tahmasp's QUINTET of Nizami, folios 2 verso and 3 recto

Ca. 1540
360 x 250 mm. (each folio)
Lent by the British Library (Or. 2265)

Noble in proportion, sumptuous in its golds, lapis lazuli, and accents of richly colored pigment, this double page combines the large-scale power of Safavid architectural ornament with the minute perfection of jewelry. If less bold and dignified than its predecessor in the *Book of Kings* (no. 3), it nonetheless invites more sustained viewing. The arabesques are more complex, finely scaled, and playfully inventive—perfectly matched to the border drawings of birds, animals, trees, and flowers. These can be attributed to Aqa-Mirak, Shah Tahmasp's closest friend among the artists, who specialized in such brilliantly improvised illumination. For another example of his work in this vein see number 52, folios 19 verso and 20 recto.

OPPOSITE PAGE: no. 49, folio 2 verso.

بسم الله الرحمن الرحیم هست کلید در گنج حکیم
فاتحهٔ فکرت و ختم سخن نام خدایست برو ختم کن
پیش وجود همه آیندگان بیش بقای همه پایندگان
سابقه سالار جهان قدم مرسله پیوند گلوی قلم
ابر گهربار ازو یافت بخش مقرعهٔ رعد و سنان درخش
سکهٔ نام جبروتش احد پایهٔ کام ملکوتش ابد
پرده گشای فلک پرده دار پردگی پرده شناسان کار

50. *Nushirvan Listening to the Owls in the Ruined Palace*

From the *Treasury of Mysteries* of Shah Tahmasp's QUINTET of Nizami, folio 15 verso

Attributable to Aqa-Mirak, assisted by Mir Sayyid-'Ali

Ca. 1540

304 x 194 mm. (miniature only)

Lent by the British Library (Or. 2265)

The first of Nizami's Five Poems, "The Treasury of Mysteries," consists of twenty discourses on theological and ethical topics, each followed by an illustrative apologue. In one such moralistic tale the Sasanian king Nushirvan and his vizier happened upon a ruined, deserted village in which two owls were hooting eerily. Disturbed by the sound, Nushirvan asked his vizier what secrets the owls were telling each other. "Forgive me for repeating what they say," he replied. "One of those birds is giving his daughter as a mate to the other, and demands from him a suitable marriage-portion. 'Give her,' he says, 'this ruined village and one or two others thrown in.' 'By all means,' replies the other. 'If our worthy sovereign persists in his present courses, and leaves his people to perish in misery and neglect, I will gladly give not two nor three, but a hundred thousand ruined villages.'" S. R. C.

Aqa-Mirak's first painting for the *Quintet* scarcely differs stylistically from his most progressive miniature for the *Book of Kings, Faridun Tests His Sons* (no. 14). In both, cascading water, ursine cliffs abounding in psychologically intriguing grotesques, entwined flowering trees, and delightful animals are almost interchangeable. *Nushirvan and the Owls*[1], however, differs in finish and mood. The former can be ascribed to long hours of work by Mir Sayyid-'Ali, whose father Mir Musavvir inscribed the wall of the ruined palace with lines interpretable as in his praise; the latter results from the unusual mood of Nizami's story—nostalgia. This inspired the artist to ponder life's ironies, and to devise cumulative symbols expressing their poignancy: a snake that slithers through the walls, already stained and weakened by water and lichens; a soulful, wraith of a puppy; and cracked ceramic tiles, their once proud design now comparable to a crone's smile, saddened by missing teeth. Atop the ruin, however, life goes on—represented by a family of cranes, one of which approaches the nest, bearing a delicious snake.

By intention, no doubt, both Shah Tahmasp's *Book of Kings* and *Quintet* open with pictures by Aqa-Mirak, his closest friend among the artists. Although outshone by Sultan-Muhammad's combination of the transcendental and the comical, Aqa-Mirak's soulful concern with imponderables stirs us as deeply, and induces serious speculation. Perhaps he was sensitively prophetic in the choice of a morality tale concerned with bad government as the opening miniature for the *Quintet* was Shah Tahmasp's last great illustrated manuscript. According to Qazi Ahmad, in about 1544/45 Shah Tahmasp "wearied of the field of calligraphy and painting [and] occupied himself with important affairs of state, with the well being of the country and the tranquility of his subjects . . ."[2]

Inscribed

on wall

Build up the desert heart of those deprived of bliss; there is no better building in this ruined world than this. Mir. . . . the Painter [Musavvir] 946 A.H. [1539/40 A.D.]

FOLLOWING PAGES: complete miniature, left, and detail, right.

1. For color reproductions, see Binyon, *The Poems of Nizami*, pl. III. Also, see Welch, *Persian Painting*, pls. 19, 20.

2. Quotation from the *Gulistān-i Hunar* [Garden of the Arts] by Qāzī Ahmad Qumi. Persian text. ed. Ahmad Suhaylī Khwānsār (Tehran: Bunyād-i Farhang-i Irān, 1352/1973).

کین ده ویران بگذاری بما نیز چنین چند سپاری بما

آن دگرش گوید ازین درگذر جور ملک بین و برو غم مخور

گر ملک اینست نه بس روزگار زین ده ویران دهمت صد هزار

در ملک این لفظ چنان درگرفت

کاه برآورد و فغان برگرفت

هر که درین خانه شبی داد کرد
خانه فردای خود آباد کرد
پیرزنی را ستمی درگرفت
دست زد و دامن سنجر گرفت
کای ملک آزرم تو کم دیده‌ام
وز تو همه ساله ستم دیده‌ام

51. *Sultan Sanjar and the Old Woman*

From the *Treasury of Mysteries* of Shah Tahmasp's QUINTET of Nizami, folio 18 recto (and facing page of text)
Attributable to Sultan-Muhammad

Ca. 1540
265 x 205 mm. (miniature only)
Lent by the British Library (Or. 2265)

When an old woman complained to Sultan Sanjar, the Seljuk ruler from 1119 to 1156, that she had been robbed by one of his soldiers, he coldly rebuffed her, claiming that the old woman's grievances were trivial in comparison to his latest military campaign. To this she replied, "What is the use of conquering foreign armies when you are unable to make your own behave?" S. R. C.

Always innovative, Sultan-Muhammad envisioned the old lady as an individual, whose bent, humble, but sturdy silhouette is a type still encountered in Iran. He contrasts her immovable strength not only with the proud Sanjar, but also with the foppish pageboy, who turns his unformed face towards hers, aghast at her presumptuousness. Vying with the central players in liveliness are the rock-spirits, such as the profile set against the tree trunk, who is at least as outspoken as the old woman, although he reprimands a mere lion. Once again, the artist has employed his favorite compositional scheme, an all-encompassing oval, suggestive of the flame of a candle. Like Aqa-Mirak's miniatures for the *Quintet*, this picture marks the trend at Shah Tahmasp's court towards an increasingly refined and naturalistic style, as was apparent already in the later miniatures for the *Shahnama.*[1]

1. For color reproductions, see Pope, *Survey of Persian Art*, vol. V, pl. 899. Also, see Binyon, *The Poems of Nizami*, pl. IV, and Welch, *Persian Painting*, pl. 21.

52. Two Folios of Calligraphy and Illumination

From Shah Tahmasp's QUINTET of Nizami, folios 19 verso and 20 recto
Border drawings attributable to Aqa-Mirak

Ca. 1540
360 x 250 mm. (each folio); ca. 215 x 130 mm. (text areas)
Lent by the British Library (Or. 2265)

Unlike the *Book of Kings*, with its simpler gold-flecked borders, the *Quintet* was enriched by border designs drawn in silver and several tones of gold. Reminiscent of the borders for the *Gulistan* of Sa'di (nos. 45, 46), these contain real and fabulous beasts set in fanciful landscapes as well as arabesques. The pair of borders included here can be ascribed to Aqa-Mirak on the basis of their animals, birds, flowers, trees, and rocks. Almost a signature is the sinuously flowing stream at the right, known from two of his outstanding miniatures (nos. 14 and 50). Noted for his ornamental drawings in gold, Aqa-Mirak was cited in Sadiki-Bek's *The Canons of Painting* for his animal-designs (*javar-sāzī*).[1]

1. See Dickson and Welch, *The Houghton Shahnameh*, Appendix.

53. *The Physicians' Duel*

From the *Treasury of Mysteries* of Shah Tahmasp's QUINTET of Nizami, folio 26 verso (and facing page of text)
Attributable to Aqa-Mirak, assisted by Mir Sayyid-'Ali

Ca. 1540
292 x 196 mm. (miniature only)
Lent by the British Library (Or. 2265)

At court two rival physicians contended in an odd medicinal duel. One offered the other a deadly pill. He swallowed it, and immediately rendered it harmless by taking a powerful antidote. He then picked a rose and, while his opponent watched apprehensively, he breathed a spell on it before handing it to his rival to smell. The latter sniffed it and fell dead. Thus, the power of fear was proved more lethal than actual poison. S. R. C.

However intricate their elaboration, Aqa-Mirak's illustrations tell their stories forcefully. Every detail is subservient to the action, and the moment depicted is chosen for fullest dramatic impact. Here, all lines converge at front stage center, where the triumphant physician claps his hands with glee, and topples his rival—a graceful corpse whose fate is symbolized by the undignified turban and the lethal rose, now fit for the dustbin.

Typical of Aqa-Mirak's compositions is the spotting of figures, still life, trees, and architectural elements over the page in a seemingly carefree but in fact thoughtfully artful arrangement. As so often in his pictures, several favored personages are among the players: the lightly mustached young man, enthroned, and the well-trimmed black-beard, who played the lead as Rustam but is now demoted to minor roles. The toothy smile we first admired in *Faridun Tests His Sons* (no. 14) now adorns the victor.

Although this miniature was fully planned, designed, and mostly painted by Aqa-Mirak, the almost compulsive fineness of detail, so gloriously successful in the treatment of the entwined trees, should be credited to Mir Sayyid-'Ali, who was unrivalled in the Safavid workshops for jewel-like finishing, and who probably resented the portion of his time spent working for others, particularly for Aqa-Mirak.[1]

Inscribed

over door

May this court always be opened in prosperity

over the pavilion

Even though the dignity of our threshold does not become lofty, nevertheless the sun sets its feet in our house. May Allah perpetuate his Kingship and the Sovereignty for ever.

1. For color reproductions, see Binyon, *The Poems of Nizami*, pl. V. Also see Welch, *Persian Painting*, pls. 22, 23.

54. *Shapur Showing the Portrait of Khusraw to Shirin* (in fact, *Nushaba Recognizing Iskandar*)

From *Khusraw and Shirin* of Shah Tahmasp's QUINTET of Nizami, folio 48 verso (and facing page of text)
Correctly ascribed to Mirza-'Ali

Ca. 1540
286 x 182 mm. (miniature only)
Lent by the British Library (Or. 2265)

Although the lines of poetry on this page refer to an episode from the story of Khusraw and Shirin, the scene itself is an illustration to the last book of the Quintet, *"The Iskandar Nama." Iskandar, known to us as Alexander the Great, had heard stories praising Nushaba, the queen of the peaceful, prosperous land of Burda. To test the truth of these tales, he decided to enter her court disguised as a messenger. Despite his ruse, Nushaba recognized him immediately. Iskandar protested, but the queen insisted that she had identified him correctly. To settle the matter, a servant brought Iskandar a piece of silk. He opened it, beheld his own portrait, and was speechless. Sensing Iskandar's fear, graceful Queen Nushaba immediately made him welcome with compliments and conciliatory wishes.*[1] S. R. C.

How differently from his father Sultan-Muhammad, Mirza-'Ali experienced life! Of the first Safavid generation, the father served Shah Isma'il, a rugged, inspired, unorthodox soldier. He would have known battles, both won and lost, the hardy life of campaigns, and hot-blooded feelings. Mirza-'Ali, on the other hand, grew up at the established Safavid court, in ateliers where the pointing of brushes and cutting of nibs mattered more than sharpening scimitars. Since his father's flexible, pioneering spirit was no longer necessary, he settled into courtly ways, and explored the sophisticated, sociable milieu of Shah Tahmasp's inner circle. Like the duc de Saint-Simon at the court of Louis XIV, he made a study of his king's friends, attendants, and hangers-on, most of whom he depicted with a psychiatrist's concern for human foibles. Characteristically, in this miniature he was at least as keen to record life at court as to illustrate the topic at hand—a point underscored by the fact that the miniature was incorrectly placed in the text some three hundred years ago, and few noted the error.[2]

1. When Prince Khusraw, son of Shah Hurmuzd, dreamed of a beautiful and talented girl named Shirin and learned from his artist-friend Shapur that a princess of that name was niece and heiress to the Queen of Armenia, he sent Shapur to Armenia to arrange for the betrothal. There, Shapur cunningly and diplomatically lured Shirin into viewing the portraits of Khusraw he had painted; and these were so compelling that she in turn fell in love with the Iranian prince.

2. For color reproductions, see Binyon, *The Poems of Nizami*, pl. VI. Also, see Welch, *Persian Painting*, pl. 24.

بیاوردند صورت پیش دلبند
در آن صورت فرو شد ساعتی چند
نه دل میداد ازو دل برگرفتن
نمی شایستش اندر بر گرفتن

55. Khusraw Watching Shirin Bathing

From *Khusraw and Shirin* of Shah Tahmasp's QUINTET of Nizami, folio 53 verso
Correctly ascribed to Sultan-Muhammad

Ca. 1540
287 x 180 mm. (miniature only)
Lent by the British Library (Or. 2265)

Khusraw, son of the Persian king Hurmuzd, dreamed he would ride the world's fastest horse, Shabdiz, and gain a sweet and beautiful wife named Shirin. Soon after, Khursraw's friend, Shapur, described his journey to Armenia where he saw the queen's ravishing niece, Shirin. Amazed, Khusraw pressed Shapur to bring Shirin to Persia. Returning to Armenia, Shapur sparked Shirin's interest by hanging portraits of Khusraw on trees and explained how she could join the prince in Persia. The next day Shirin mounted Shabdiz and rode towards Persia. After fourteen days and nights, exhausted and covered with dust, she came to a gentle pool and stopped to bathe.

Khusraw, meanwhile, had been forced to flee Persia. In his haste he had even outstripped his companions when he came upon a sparkling pool in which a lovely woman was bathing. Astounded by her beauty, Khusraw quietly drew closer. Startled, Shirin hid herself in her long tresses, dressed, and rode off. Although Khusraw desired the exquisite maiden for his own, he never guessed her identity. Nor did Shirin recognize Khusraw, though later she wondered if the handsome horseman was the prince. S. R. C.

To please his patron's taste for detail, Sultan-Muhammad has colored each leaf, twist of hair, and stone in this scintillating scene with a jeweler's artifice. One suspects, however, that the artist was more happily matched to his earlier patron, Shah Isma'il, than to the increasingly orthodox Tahmasp. Still, Sultan-Muhammad's sense of comedy and innate flexibility not only enabled him to survive but to continue growing artistically, as his earth-spirits show. In the *Court of the Gayumars* (no.8), these spirits almost leap from the page, suggesting Shah Isma'il's state of mind rather than Tahmasp's. In the *Death of Zuhhak* (no. 13) they seem tamer, exchanging fewer cosmic jokes. Here they are yet more restrained and harder to find, but they can still be seen in the rocks around Shirin's pool, as evocative as ever. In the proportions of his figures, the artist still values expressiveness above naturalism.[1] Khusraw, far more tightly and finely painted than *Rustam* (no. 2) or the lurching drunk (no. 44), is scarcely more normal in canon. Rising in the saddle like the sun at dawn, his shoulders loom vast and powerful, but his legs would serve a midget.

1. For color reproductions, see Pope, *Survey of Persian Art*, vol. V, pl. 898. Also, see Binyon, *The Poems of Nizami*, pl. VII, and Welch, *Persian Painting*, pl. 25.

در آب نیلگون چون گل نشسته
پرند نیلگون تا ناف بسته
ز هر سو شاخ گیسو شانه می کرد
بنفشه بر سر گل دانه می کرد

56. Shapur Returning to Khusraw

From *Khusraw and Shirin* of Shah Tahmasp's QUINTET of Nizami, folio 57 verso
Correctly ascribed to Aqa-Mirak

Ca. 1540
295 x 200 mm. (miniature only)
Lent by the British Library (Or. 2265)

Following their encounter at the pool, Shirin and Khusraw proceeded in opposite directions, she to Persia, he to Armenia. After languishing in the Persian palace for weeks with no word from Khusraw, Shirin requested that a palace be built for her in a mountain plain. But to spite her, Khusraw's jealous servants built it in a sweltering site where Shirin sadly awaited Khusraw's return. In Armenia Shirin's aunt, the queen, greeted Khusraw and lavished food, drink, and entertainment upon him. One night in the midst of this revelry Shapur appeared at Khusraw's tent and recounted his discovery of Shirin, the showing of Khusraw's portrait to her, her departure for Persia, and his belief that by now she had reached Khusraw's palace. Joyfully, Khusraw sent Shapur to bring her to him in Armenia. S. R. C.

Boldly designed, as one expects of a work of Aqa-Mirak, this picture is less finely finished than his first two miniatures for the *Quintet*. In every detail it bears his stamp, from the precariously massed whites of the tents, skillfully kept in balance, to the idealized portrayal of the Shah as Khusraw, and the realistic catching of gestures in mid-motion, as though by a fast camera shutter. We miss, however, the minutiae of detail seen in Aqa-Mirak's first two paintings for the *Quintet*; this superb finish we attribute to Mir Sayyid-'Ali. By now, it appears, he was released from such labors, undoubtedly to his great relief, and possibly to the distress of Aqa-Mirak (who may, on the other hand, have urged that he now be accepted as a full-fledged master).[1]

1. For a color reproduction, see Binyon, *The Poems of Nizami*, pl. VIII.

ملک سرمست و ساقی باده در دست
که بر در بار خواهد جست شاپور
نوای بلبلان چون مطرب مست
چه فرمایی درآید یا شود دور
درآمد گلرخی چون سرو آزاد
ز دلداران چو سرو و با دل شاد
ز شادی خواست جستن خسرو از جای
بفرمودش درآوردن به درگاه
وگر نه عقل باشد کار فرمای
ز دل گرمی بجوش آمد دل شاه

57. Khusraw Enthroned

From *Khusraw and Shirin* of Shah Tahmasp's QUINTET of Nizami, folio 60 verso
Correctly ascribed to Aqa-Mirak

Ca. 1540
290 x 182 mm. (miniature only)
Lent by the British Library (Or. 2265)

When Shapur reached Shirin in Persia, she was so overjoyed to see him and to learn that Khusraw was in Armenia that they set out immediately for the palace of Shirin's aunt. Before Shirin and Khusraw could be united, however, Khusraw heard that his father had died and rushed back to Persia to claim the throne. Once again he had missed his beloved Shirin. Dutifully, but alone, Khusraw remained in Persia, a just sovereign to his contented subjects. S. R. C.

Aqa-Mirak's miniatures are predominantly two dimensional in their rendering of space. He usually avoided architecture, perhaps because he preferred sinuous or curving lines to straight ones. Characteristically, his facade here is as insubstantial as a house of cards, and the figures on the roof seem propped up, as though in a stage setting. Khusraw and his forty courtiers and attendants are arranged according to the artist's favorite method, in a buoyantly staccato pattern that lends cheeriness to a festive occasion.[1]

If we missed the loving finish of Mir Sayyid-'Ali in *Shapur Returning to Khusraw* (no. 56), its absence is now less disconcerting. Apparently, the master was happy again to depend upon his own resources.

1. For a color reproduction, see Binyon, *The Poems of Nizami*, pl. IX.

دلش گرچه به شیرین مبتلا بود
بترک مملکت گفتن خطا بود

58. *Khusraw and Shirin Listening to Stories Told by Shirin's Maids*

From *Khusraw and Shirin* of Shah Tahmasp's QUINTET of Nizami, folio 66 verso (and facing page of text)
Correctly ascribed to Aqa-Mirak

Ca. 1540
300 x 180 mm. (miniature only)
Lent by the British Library (Or. 2265)

Although Khusraw governed with justice, a treacherous general conspired against him and forced him to flee Persia. Again he saddled his horse and rode at top speed towards Armenia. Upon reaching the environs of the Armenian capital, he decided to relax and go hunting. By chance, Shirin and her companions had set out to hunt that same day. And at last, in a clearing, Khusraw and Shirin met. Each was struck dumb by the other's beauty and magnificence. After retiring to the Armenian castle, the lovers spent their days and nights courting, feasting, and sitting side by side. To preserve Shirin's virtue until she and Khusraw were married, the queen forbade the lovers to be left to themselves. Every evening musicians played and sang for them, unless, as in this painting, Shirin's maidens recited love poetry and told stories. Despite the merry-making and Khusraw's entreaties, Shirin guarded her chastity. Moreover, she urged Khusraw to regain his kingdom before making her his wife. In due course he left her in order to fight the usurper, Bahram Chubina, and win back his throne (see no. 66).[1]

S. R. C.

Aqa-Mirak usually avoided symmetry. In this miniature, he put himself to the task of making it interesting. Although Shirin and her maids are neatly arranged facing Khusraw and his courtiers, with the throne, pool, and portico set on a rigid axis, a lantern-bearer in the foreground, like a rock tossed in a tranquil pond, upsets the cool balance. Further dissonant chords are struck by the figure in the garden, left rear, and a pair of ducks which overbalance the single one on the right. But all these weighty forms, like the white tents in *Shapur Returning to Khusraw*, have been balanced in Aqa-Mirak's artistic juggling act. Khusraw's plumed turban, his courtiers standing in the right foreground, and a second torch-bearer, in front of the fence at the right, provide perfect compensation.

The artist's notion of feminine beauty is evident here, despite the "improvement," by Muhammad Zaman in the seventeenth century, of several of Shirin's maids. Curiously, Shirin and the unretouched maids are upsettingly low of brow. Should we ascribe this to a Safavid vogue? To the artist's preference for the bovine? Or to a somewhat misogynistic sense of humor?

Inscribed

over steps *O thou who art the one who controls the throne of Jamshid, may all the world be thine.*

over throne
The pupil of my eye is thy dwelling. Show kindness and come down, for the house is thy house.

on back of throne *By happy omen. . . . the disposition of Khusraw. . . . the throne of Khusraw*

1. For color reproductions, see Pope, *Survey of Persian Art*, vol. V, pl. 896. Also see Binyon, *The Poems of Nizami*, pl. X.

قران مشتری با زهره پیوست
چو آمد در سخن نوبت بشاپور
سخن را تازه کرد از عشق منشور
که شیرین انگبینی بود در جام

59. *Khusraw Listening to Barbad Playing the Lute*

From *Khusraw and Shirin* of Shah Tahmasp's QUINTET of Nizami, folio 77 verso
Correctly ascribed to Mirza-'Ali

Ca. 1540
306 x 182 mm. (miniature only)
Lent by the British Library (Or. 2265)

To regain the Persian throne, Khusraw made a treaty with the Byzantine emperor: in exchange for the support of the Byzantine armies Khusraw agreed to marry Maryam, the emperor's daughter. Khusraw's coronation ceremonies were followed at once by wedding festivities. One fateful night after too much wine Khusraw summoned his favorite minstrel, Barbad, to entertain the revelers. The bard sang thirty songs about the love of Khusraw for Shirin—songs so moving that Khusraw lavished gifts on the singer, and in a fit of emotion told Maryam to take Shirin as her slave. Maryam refused, and swore to kill Shirin on sight.

In Mirza-'Ali's painting of Barbad singing, the nurse with a child and the boy with an arrow may allude to Khusraw's future death.[1] *For an evil male child named Shiruya was born to him and Maryam. Although Khusraw and Shirin eventually married, Khusraw's life was cut short by the successful assassination plot of Shiruya. Shirin stabbed herself and bled to death over her lover's body, united with him at last.* S. R. C.

Mirza-'Ali's figures stand, sit, and move more articulately and convincingly than those by any other Safavid painter, a symptom of his intense concern for people. If his father explored earth and heaven, he, more narrowly, but fascinatingly, concentrated upon mankind. The same objective study of anatomy that enabled him to depict the man intermeshed with gate and fences in the left foreground, made him an accurate observer of Safavid graces and disgraces. These he recorded with true to life textures and proportions until the 1550s and later, when even he—a classicist by nature—yielded to the taste for mannerism. But even then, his figures were drawn with understanding of volume, weight, and balance; and as before, their individuality was analyzed with sympathy and respect (see nos. 78, 82, 83 and 85).

Miniatures such as *Khusraw Listening to Barbad* are in fact group portraits, in which each figure seems to have been based upon someone at the Shah's court. Invariably, his characterizations are enlivened by telling poses, often in chit-chatting pairs. Close study of gestures and faces exposes all manner of subplots, suggestive of political intrigue, or topics for a psychoanalyst's case book, or a gossip column.

If Mirza-'Ali delved into the machinations of the Shah's inner circle, he also felt warmly towards the harem, with its ladies, nurses, and children. *Nushirvan Receives an Embassy*

OPPOSITE PAGE: Detail of no. 59.

from the King of Hind, his most progressive painting for the *Shahnama* and a precursor of the present painting, also carries us into those closed precincts. [2]

Inscribed

over pavilion

May this festive assembly be as rain to the garden and may the light of the countenance of the Shah be bright. From the dome of the heavens, as long as the sun and moon exist, may the assembly be adorned with the person of the Shah.

around the carpet

With the furnishing of your two eyes you make a bridal chamber of that dwelling. In every place you travel you wish to make the dust into a road there. How pleasant. . . . with one another.

OPPOSITE PAGE: no. 59.

1. For other color plates, see Binyon, *The Poems of Nizami*, pl. XI; and Welch, *Persian Painting*, pls. 26, 27.

2. See Welch, *A King's Book of Kings*, pp. 180–183

گر او را سپهری کو سر گرم شد رای — نسب داران کو سر ماند بر جای
گر او را فیض رحمت کش ساقی — جهان وارثانش باد باقی

گر او را داد خاک از تخته بندی — [illegible] تخت گیر ازا گزندی
گر او بی تاج شد تا بخش رضا باد — پسران تاجدار ازابقا باد

خصوصا وارث اعمار شاهان — نظرگاه دعای نیک خواهان
مؤید نصرة الدین کآفرینش — زنام او پذیرد نور بینش

پناه خسروان اعظم اتابک — فریدون وار بر عالم مبارک
بشاهی تاج بخش تاجداران — بدولت یادگار شهریاران

بدانایش هفت اختر شکرخند — بمولاییش نه گردون کمربند
ستاره پایه بخت بلندش — فلک را بوسه گه سم سمندش

سپهر پرش باد در کشور خدایی — وثیقت نامه کشور کشایی
جهان را تا ابد شاه جهان باد — بدانچه امید دارد کامران باد

سعادت یار او در کامرانی — مساعد با سعادت زندگانی
سخن را بر سعادت ختم کردم — ورق کاینجا رساندم درنوردم

روانش باد جفت شادکامی
که گوید باد رحمت بر نظامی

تمت الکتاب بعون الملک الوهاب علی ید احقر العباد
شاه محمود النیشابوری غفر الله ذنوبه وستر عیوبه فی سلخ
شهر ربیع الاول سنه سبع واربعین وتسعمایه الهجریة النبویه

60. Peony Arabesque

From Shah Tahmasp's QUINTET of Nizami, folio 128 recto

Ca. 1540
360 x 250 mm. (folio size)
Lent by the British Library (Or. 2265)

This seeming trifle is one of the unique small delights of the *Quintet*—indeed, of all Safavid ornament. Like a few of Chopin's *bagatelles*, it soars beyond the limitations of "minor" art, and in the *Quintet*, provides a seductive change of pace. Through the scrolling graces of flowering vines, we sense one of art's rarest and most appealing moods, bittersweet poignancy. Its deceptively easy, tripping line, Turkman-inspired blossoms, and broken stems suggest the hand of a major artist at work, one to whom this illumination provided a stimulatingly fresh challenge. The border typifies those added when the manuscript was refurbished during the late seventeenth century.

61. *Majnun Brought in Chains by the Old Woman to Layla's Tent*

From *Layla and Majnun* of Shah Tahmasp's QUINTET of Nizami, folio 157 verso (and facing page of text)
Correctly ascribed to Mir Sayyid-'Ali

Ca. 1540
320 x 182 mm. (miniature only).
Lent by the British Library (Or. 2265)

Set in Arabia, the story of Layla and Majnun began when two children, Qays and Layla, met in school and fell in love. Soon their schoolmates taunted the lovestruck Qays with the name "Majnun," or "madman," and when Layla's father heard of Majnun's love for Layla he became so incensed that he withdrew her from school. Distracted by her absence, Majnun fled to the desert where he repeatedly murmured Layla's name and composed love songs for her which came to be sung throughout Arabia. Despite Majnun's father's efforts to ease his sorrow, Majnun remained in the desert obsessed with Layla.

One day an old woman dragging a man in chains approached Majnun, who asked why he was so treated. The old woman explained that he was a dervish who travelled with her through the desert to help beg for food. Majnun persuaded the old woman to free the dervish and chain him instead, in exchange for all the food they would receive. Henceforth, the old woman and Majnun wandered through the desert from village to village. One day they came to a familiar camp. Majnun recognized Layla's tent and was seized with a fit of madness. He cried out her name, broke his chains, and fled back to the desert.[1] S. R. C.

Less concerned with formal court subjects than Mirza-'Ali, Mir Sayyid-'Ali was particularly fond of rustic scenes, which he translated into appropriately royal terms. This strong composition, probably inspired by Sultan-Muhammad's *Tur Beheads Iraj* (no. 15), is an arrangement of maids at work, shepherds with their flocks, unruly ragamuffins, and assorted domestic scenes, as well as the portrayal of an incident in Majnun's tragedy. One suspects that Mir Sayyid-'Ali preferred such company to the denizens of court and the accuracy with which he rendered them argues that he spent many hours sketching in the field. The humbler the station of his subject, the livelier and more intimate his depiction. Although he painted great courtiers with every bauble or hair defined, his shepherds are more convincing, and he was still more successful when drawing animals.

Sadly, his marvelous compositions are inhabited by a strangely silent race, who rarely, if ever, communicate with one another, either through words or eyes. Most of his figures gaze ahead, their eyes unfocused. Despite this revealing limitation, which tends to reduce humanity to still life, Mir Sayyid-'Ali must be ranked with the major Safavid artists. Only Bihzad himself, at the peak of his career, painted more meticulously or lovingly.

1. For color reproductions, see Pope, *Survey of Persian Art*, vol. V, pl. 910. Also, see Binyon, *The Poems of Nizami*, pl. XII and Welch, *Persian Painting*, pls. 28, 29.

هر وحش که بود در
و شده شتابان
از شیر و گوزن و گرگ و روباه
لشکرگاهی کشیده در راه
ایشان همه گشته بنده فرمان
او بر همه شاه چون سلیمان

62. *Majnun with the Animals in the Desert*

From *Layla and Majnun* of Shah Tahmasp's QUINTET of Nizami, folio 166 recto (and facing page of text)
Correctly ascribed to Aqa-Mirak

Ca. 1540
300 x 207 mm. (miniature only)
Lent by the British Library (Or. 2265)

When Majnun returned to the desert all the wild animals flocked to him. Every day Majnun and his animals scoured the desert for roots and herbs, and every evening they gathered around Majnun to hear his love songs for Layla, their heads bowed. Majnun was particularly fond of one fawn, whose dark eyes reminded him of Layla. In the painting he fondles and kisses this gentle substitute for his beloved. S. R. C.

Of all the episodes in the tale of Layla and Majnun, this is probably the most picturesque, and among the hundreds of painted versions, Aqa-Mirak's is outstanding for sheer beauty and pathetic sweetness. The tender sympathy between Majnun and the animals, his emaciated but sensitive body, and the suitably pale colors of the lansdcape, flowing like honey-thick lava, compose an unforgettable image.[1] Always keen on animal painting, Aqa-Mirak has gathered an engaging zoological garden containing the sausage-like ibex also seen in *Rustam Finds Kay Qubad* (no. 19). Both pictures likewise include the only instances known to us in Safavid painting of the Chinese symbol for Yin and Yang, found as whorls of hair on Rustam's tiger-skin and on the living animal that turns away goggle-eyed from Majnun's temptingly delicious deer.

Detail of no. 62.

1. For color reproductions, see Binyon, *The Poems of Nizami*, pl. XIII; and Welch, *Persian Painting*, pls. 30, 31.

چون محمد ز جبرئیل براز
گوش کرد آن پیام روح نواز
زان سخن هوش را تمامی داد
گوش را حلقهٔ غلامی داد
آن امین خدای در تنزیل
وین امین خرد بعقل دلیل

63. *The Ascent of the Prophet to Heaven*

From the *Seven Portraits* of Shah Tahmasp's QUINTET of Nizami, folio 195 recto (and facing page of text)
Attributable to Sultan-Muhammad

Ca. 1540
287 x 186 mm. (miniature only)
Lent by the British Library (Or. 2265)

Traditionally Persian poets dedicated their works not only to actual patrons but also to God, to whom they directed prayers for inspiration. Often these prayers were accompanied by a description of the Miraj, or the nocturnal ascent of the Prophet Muhammad astride the half-human horse Buraq, to the Seventh Heaven. Nizami's lines conjure up the speed of the journey into the heavens and the brilliant light of the sky before Muhammad enters into the presence of God:

"And from his moon-light brilliancy he drew a veil of mercury o'er Venus fair.
Ascending to the throne-room of the sky, he crowned the sun's head with a golden crown."

S. R. C.

Ultimately, it is not skill, or talent, or virtuosity that identifies a great artist, but profundity of spirit; and the rarest, most elevating works of art are visionary. In Persianate painting, Sultan-Muhammad's pictures, whether of tipplers, demons, or Shahs, invariably reach beyond their subject matter. His *Rustam Sleeping* (no. 2), *Allegory of Drunkenness* (no. 44), and *Court of Gayumars* (no. 8) transcend earthly experience. *The Ascent of the Prophet*, probably his final masterpiece, unites the artist's personal, spiritual vision with a profound religious theme. The vibrant oval seen in all his most serious pictures is now composed of ecstatic angels, heavenly clouds, and stars; and in its eye, the Prophet soars heavenward, radiant within a flaming aura.

This majestic picture[1] is scarcely marred by the "European" faces of angels, upper left, presumably repainted by Muhammad Zaman. Like a shaft of light, the miniature illuminates, and one must stand back from its spiritual heat to observe art historical evidence: the familiar "Caucasian" profile of the angel bearing an offering of flame, whom we have encountered before in the *Celebration of 'Id* (no. 43) and in *The Court of Gayumars* (no. 8), and the lingering appearance in another angel's hat, center foreground, of Turkman foliage. Inasmuch as Sultan-Muhammad must have been born in the later 1470s or early 1480s, and died in about 1550, this picture, as one would expect from its combination of technical perfection and wisdom, was his penultimate flowering.

OPPOSITE PAGE: Detail of no. 63.

1. For color reproductions, see Pope, *Survey of Persian Art*, vol. V, pl. 897. Also see, Binyon, *The Poems of Nizami*, pl. XIV; and Welch, *Persian Painting*, pls. 32, 33.

64. *Bahram Gur Exhibiting his Hunting Prowess by Shooting an Ass and a Lion with One Arrow before Fitna*

From the *Seven Portraits* of Shah Tahmasp's QUINTET of Nizami, folio 202 verso
Correctly ascribed to Sultan-Muhammad

Ca. 1540
300 x 187 mm. (miniature only)
Lent by the British Library (Or. 2265)

According to the Persian court astrologers, Prince Bahram would have a happy life if he were brought up in Yemen and he was sent there. As he matured, Bahram gained a reputation throughout Arabia as a hunter of enormous skill. One day Bahram happened upon a lion tearing the back off a wild ass. Drawing his bow, he released the arrow and skewered both animals through their shoulders into the ground. This feat so astonished Bahram's companions that they nicknamed him "Bahram Gur"—or Bahram of the wild ass. At the behest of the king of Yemen the episode was painted on the walls of Bahram's house. The work was so successful that viewers believed the lion and ass were not mere pictures but actually living animals. S. R. C.

Sultan-Muhammad's characterizations, including earth-beings, storm our senses and feelings. This picture compels us to hear the growls and cries of animals, to wince as the arrows strike home, and to share the huntsmen's excitement when bowstrings twang. Even oft-repeated motifs, such as the Turkman bear hurling a rock at a confidently indestructible lion-spirit, were lent breath by the artist, whose miniatures invariably stem from direct responses to nature as well as from earlier art. This insistent combination is especially apparent in the Stubbs-like lion and ass, an ancient motif given new impact by the artist's grasp of anatomy. Although the lion's mask is formulaic, the texture of fur and musculature of the haunches seem drawn from life.[1]

1. For a color reproduction, see Binyon, *The Poems of Nizami*, pl. XV.

65. *Bahram Gur Pinning an Ass's Hoof to its Ear with One Arrow to Prove his Prowess to Fitna*

From the *Seven Portraits* of Shah Tahmasp's QUINTET of Nizami, folio 211 recto
Correctly ascribed to Muzaffar-'Ali

Ca. 1540
303 x 182 mm. (miniature only)
Lent by the British Library (Or. 2265)

After the death of his father, Bahram returned to Persia to claim the throne. As in Yemen he rode to the hunt, frequently accompanied by Fitna, a beautiful female musician. While Bahram pursued game, Fitna played her harp. One day Fitna piqued Bahram by failing to praise his hunting prowess. When Bahram asked Fitna how she thought he should kill a wild ass, she challenged him to pin its hoof to its ear. Without hesitation Bahram sighted an ass, grazed its ear with an arrow, and when the animal lifted its hoof to scratch he shot an arrow through both ear and hoof. Even this feat was met with a taunting remark. Enraged at Fitna's response, Bahram ordered her put to death. S. R. C.

Only an Iranian artist could make bloodshed lyrical; and this transmutation was a specialty of Muzaffar-'Ali. The depiction of bounding, seemingly dancing animals was second nature to him (see no. 25). His thinly pigmented, swift brushwork lent buoyancy to everything it touched. Like the two asses here, Muzaffar-'Ali's flowers, foliage, and people are light to the point of evanescence. At first sight baffling and difficult to appreciate, his earlier paintings, including this one, lack the technical brilliance associated with Shah Tahmasp's court painters. His compositions seem loosely organized, their workmanship is skimpy, and figures are ungainly, with oddly tilted necks and spaghetti-thin fingers. Even the animals, his strong point, defy close inspection. But his miniatures rise above their deficiencies, powered by spirit alone. They spur our imaginations and invite poetic speculation. In this example, for instance, we see the rivulet beneath the tree as a symbol of the ass's mortal wound, and the blossoms it nourishes allay the animal's death agony.[1]

1. For a color reproduction, see Binyon, *The Poems of Nizami*, pl. XVI.

نهاده تخت شه بر پشت پیلی
کشیده تیغ گرد اگرد میلی
بزرگ امید پیش پیل سرمست
نظر میکرد و آن فرصت همی جست
بساعت پنجی اصطرلاب در دست
که بازار مخالف کی شود پست
993

66. *The Battle Between Khusraw and Bahram Chubina*

From Shah Tahmasp's QUINTET of Nizami, stray folio
Attributable to Mir Sayyid-'Ali

Ca. 1540
360 x 250 mm. (folio size)
Lent by the Royal Scottish Museum, Edinburgh (1896–70)

Following the death of his father, Hurmuzd, Khusraw returned to Iran and ascended the throne, while Shapur journeyed to Armenia with Shirin (see nos. 54–59). At this point, Bahram Chubina attacked the young Shah in full force, a disaster not without compensations. For Khusraw fled to Armenia, where he joined his beloved Shirin. Torn between love for her and pride, he soon accepted the responsibility of a second battle against Bahram, in which he was encouraged by both Shirin and the emperor of Rum (Byzantium), who outfitted a mighty army for him. In this picture, Khusraw, mounted on a war elephant, has just received word from Buzurjamid that the auspicious moment to attack Bahram Chubina has come. The fray has begun; corpses already litter the field. Fortunately, the veteran counsellor had read his astrolabe correctly. Khusraw won the day. Bahram fled to China and was slain. Upon hearing the news of his arch-enemy's death, Khusraw lamented the passing of a brave man.

The lessons of Aqa-Mirak and Sultan-Muhammad largely had been absorbed by the time Mir Sayyid-'Ali painted this battle scene, which owes so much to *Qaran Slays Barman* (no.18). Whole passages, showing cavaliers on horses, have been modified from the earlier miniature upon which Mir Sayyid-'Ali seemed to have worked as a brilliant apprentice. Comparison of the two compositions, however, underscores the younger artist's dependence upon archaisms. While Sultan-Muhammad's design gains immediacy and unity by the deployment of figures and animals as though seen by a swooping bird, Mir Sayyid-'Ali's is old-fashioned, and less involving. Each element is flat as a paper cut-out, and spatial depth is unconvincingly suggested by overlapping and placing more distant motifs higher on the picture plane.[1]

Mir Sayyid-'Ali's extraordinary capabilities are also apparent. His genius for two-dimensional design, for devising stunning arabesques, his sharp-eyed renderings of arms and armor, and his almost inconceivably fine craftsmanship are all displayed for our delight.[2]

1. B. W. Robinson first identified this miniature as a missing folio from the *Quintet*, and discussed it and related pages in *Persian Miniature Painting from Collections in the British Isles* (London: Victoria and Albert Museum, 1967) pp. 55–56.

2. For a color reproduction, see Gray, *Persian Painting*, p. 134.

OPPOSITE PAGE: Detail of no. 67.
Complete miniature at right.

67. *Nomadic Encampment*

From Shah Tahmasp's QUINTET of Nizami, stray folio
Correctly ascribed to Mir Sayyid-'Ali

Ca. 1540
278 x 193 mm. (miniature only)
Lent by the Fogg Art Museum, Gift of John Goelet, formerly in the Collection of Louis J. Cartier (1958.75)

This is Mir Sayyid-'Ali's most extraordinary painting, one which invites us to explore every millimeter to relish the teeming microcosm of people, animals, flowers, and precisely analyzed still-life.[1] Nothing escaped his notice. The elegant laundress, upper right, rinses cloth wetted with silver flecks. The canteen suspended from a tent pole, right center, could be duplicated, so accurately is it rendered. For the study of textiles there is no more explicit contemporary source. But if Mir Sayyid-'Ali portrayed every texture and design of the tribal carpets, the magnificient tent, center left, adorned with simurghs and arabesques, must be an original design, and it would be very surprising if this great master of ornament had not served the Shah by supplying patterns for weavers as well as by painting.

Informative as well as beautiful, this miniature reminds us that the Safavid court lived in tents for long stretches of time. When not campaigning against Uzbeks or Ottomans, or quelling their own troublesome factions, they took to the field for hunting. Artists accompanied the royal party, and this portrayal of outdoor life is an accurate, if slightly idealized, description of characteristic Safavid activities.[2]

1. B. W. Robinson has suggested that this "camp-scene with a family council in progress" illustrates an episode in the story of Layla and Majnun. See Robinson, *Persian Miniature Painting from Collections in the British Isles*, p. 55.

2. For a color reproduction, see Ernst J. Grube, *The World of Islam* (New York and Toronto: McGraw Hill, 1966) p. 127. For a detail in color, see Stuart Cary Welch, *The Art of Mughal India* (New York: The Asia Society Inc., 1964) pl. 1.

68. *Night-time in a Palace*

From Shah Tahmasp's QUINTET of Nizami, stray folio
Attributable to Mir Sayyid-'Ali

Ca. 1540
283 x 200 mm. (miniature only)
Lent by the Fogg Art Museum, Gift of John Goelet, formerly in the Collection of Louis J. Cartier (1958.76)

Although Shah Tahmasp's artists rarely signed their work, they provided convenient clues for its identification. In the earliest picture we can assign to the Mir (no. 20), we noted the hook-nosed, usually open-mouthed personage, who appears very frequently in his work. Seemingly a portrait of someone close to the artist, he is shown in many roles, and at various ages, but his profile always is unmistakable. Here he is grandfatherly, silhouetted against a doorway, conversing with a boy (upper right). In the Edinburgh *Battle Scene* (no. 66), we encounter him as a somewhat younger warrior, near the lower right margin, and in the *Nomadic Encampment*, he is a middle-aged man near the top of the miniature, talking animatedly with a youth.

As usual, Mir Sayyid-'Ali composed this miniature as a series of lovingly elaborated, flat sections, arranged in compartments as a meaningful whole. Like most artists, he repeated favorite passages, always with intriguing variations. Thus, the salivating, hennaed dog (top center) is also found in the foreground of *Majnun Brought in Chains* (no. 61). If, as we suspect, this charming pet was the artist's, the fact that he is seen as a puppy in the latter picture suggests that it was painted earlier, before the hound matured.[1]

Inscribed

in upper part of picture, over portal of mosque

"He who builds a mosque for God, God will build for him a dwelling in Paradise." This saying is an *hadīth*; for citations of where it may be found in the various *hadīth* collections, see A. J. Wensinck, *Concordance et Indices de la Tradition Musulmane,* 7 vols., (Leiden: Brill, 1936) vol. 1 p. 221. We are grateful to Peter Heath for this identification as well as for the translation.

in lower left of picture

"The pupil of my eye is your nesting place; be kind, alight, for it is your house." This is the first line of a poem from the *Dīvān* of Hafiz; for it and the rest of the poem, see: Hafiz, *Dīvān-i-Khwāja Hāfiz-i-Shirāzī*, ed. Abu'l-Qāsim Anjavī (Tehran, 1967) pp. 28–29.

1. For a color reproduction of this painting, see Grube, *The World of Islam,* p. 126.

لطف تو انیس مستمندان
قهر تو هلاک زورمندان
گر لطف کنی وگر کنی قهر
در هر دو ز رحمتت بود بهر

69. *Bahram Gur and the Shepherd Who Hanged his Dog for Allowing a Wolf to Steal the Sheep*

Perhaps a preparatory drawing for a copy of the *Seven Portraits* of the QUINTET of Nizami
Attributable to Mirza-'Ali

Ca. 1540
450 x 295 mm. (with borders)
Lent by the Museum of Fine Arts, Boston, Income of Bartlett Fund and Special Contribution (14.589)

Nizami's Seven Portraits *tells of Bahram Gur and the stories recounted by his seven princesses, each of whom occupied a separate, appropriately colored pavilion. At the time of his visit to the princess of the Seventh Clime in her white pavilion he was troubled by a malevolent vizier, upon whose deeds the princess's tale shed light. She told of a king who sought relaxation by venturing alone into the countryside, where he chanced upon a disturbing sight, a sheep dog bound and hanging from a tree. The shepherd explained that the dog had seemed a loyal keeper of the flocks, until sheep mysteriously disappeared, one by one. Puzzled by these losses, he kept careful watch and learned that the once faithful dog was making love with a female wolf, whose nightly bribe was a fine fat sheep! On hearing this rustic drama, Bahram Gur realized that his vizier and the sheep dog had much in common, and he meted out a comparable punishment to the human malefactor.*

Few large working drawings have survived from Shah Tahmasp's ateliers. This one, as has been suggested by B. W. Robinson "may, perhaps, be a rejected design for Tahmasp's Nizami"[1]—or, indeed, the actual under-drawing for an intended painting. On stylistic grounds, it can be assigned to Mirza-'Ali during the years of the *Quintet*. The handling of space, figural and facial types, water, rocks, and the shape of the turban, as worn by Bahram Gur, all point to his hand.

Beginning with a brush and thinned black ink, the artist sketched in the composition, gradually refining its elements more decisively, in darker strokes. Errors were correctable by covering them with white pigment. Less proficient painters, ranked as colorers rather than designers, either worked over sketches provided by their superiors, or built up compositions by using pounces—tracings pricked in transparent gazelle skin, through which powdered black pigment was rubbed. Major masters, such as Mirza-'Ali in his maturity, seldom, if ever, resorted to such technical crutches.

1. Robinson, *Persian Miniature Painting from Collections in the British Isles*, p. 55. A later, weaker drawing, partly copied or traced from this one is in the British Museum. See Ivan V. Stchoukine, *Les Peintures des manuscrits safavis de 1502 à 1587* (Paris: Institut Français d'archéologie de Beyrouth, 1959) pl. XXXIV.

از کف جودت که دریای کرم زو قطره ایست
در بگوشش بحر اگر گویند نمی آید گران

70. *Seated Princess with a Spray of Flowers*

Attributable to Mirza-'Ali

Ca. 1540
178 x 103 mm. (miniature only)
Lent by the Fogg Art Museum, Gift of John Goelet, formerly in the Collection of Louis J. Cartier (1958.60)

Few schools of painting in the world outshone the elegance of Safavid portraiture, and among Tabriz examples, this aristocratic princess is unequalled. A larger, more elaborate version of Mirza-'Ali's Nushaba in the *Quintet* (no. 54), she is at once seductive and unapproachably royal, perfectly mannered, without stiffness, formally aloof, yet friendly. Her eyes are focused but avoid contact, and she smiles infectiously, as though genuinely amused by some courtly *bon mot*. Despite the idealization of her moon-faced beauty, we sense her humanity. She is breathingly alive. Among Safavid artists only Mirza-'Ali could have conveyed the volume and weight of her body, and only he could have arranged her trunk and limbs so convincingly in three dimensions, with such suggestive implications to the undulating hem of her fur-lined robe with its tucks, and folds. In one of the most inspired passages of Safavid painting, flowers, curving fingers, and sinuous arabesque converge in a perfectly harmonious triad.[1]

1. For a color reproduction, see Pope, *Survey of Persian Art*, vol. V. pl. 902.

71. *Young Man Holding Flowers*

Attributable to Muzaffar-'Ali

Ca. 1540

484 x 254 mm. (with border)

Lent by the Museum of Fine Arts, Boston, Francis Bartlett Donation of 1912 and Picture Fund (14.590)

As in Muzaffar-'Ali's illustration to the *Quintet* (no. 25), the spirit of this portrait makes up for its formal deficiencies. If the hands lack precision and seem too boneless to grasp a flower, and if the legs and trunk are anatomically and structurally unarticulated, these are small matters compared to the picture's overall grace and dignity. Imposing in scale, springy in stance, and exuding happy innocence, the young man exemplifies Muzaffar-'Ali's ability to filter out all that is worldly, leaving behind only poetic essences. A counterpart to this engaging young man, with his metaphorically bow-shaped eyebrows, rides a dappled horse near the right edge of the artist's hunting scene.

Muzaffar-'Ali's technical proficiency increased over the years, and miniatures we attribute to him in the Freer Gallery of Art's *Haft Awrang* (Seven Thrones) of Jami of 1556–1565, while exhibiting all the characteristics apparent in earlier works, reveal increased mastery of brush handling and delineation.

72. Mirza-Muhammad Qabahat Offers a Letter

By 'Abd ul-Aziz

Ca. 1540
202 x 125 mm. (with border)
Private Collection

This decorous portrait of a youngish man holding a letter is inscribed (on the letter and above) with the names of both subject and artist, the two principals in a notorious court scandal. The subject, Mirza-Muhammad Qabahat, son of the royal surgeon, was a favorite pageboy of the Shah. The artist, 'Abd ul-'Aziz, the Shah's own master in painting, lured the youth away from court and stole the royal seal, with which he forged documents to smooth their escape southward. They were caught and returned to the Shah, who imprisoned Mirza-Qabahat, but soon ordered his release. The artist fared worse. He forfeited his nose and ears—and according to some, the enraged Shah himself performed the surgery. 'Abd ul-'Aziz, now dubbed "Clipped-ears," whittled and polychromed a prosthetic nose said to have been an improvement upon nature's original.

The portrait was painted after the young man had outlived the first bloom of youth and passions had cooled. On grounds of costume, style, and border, it can be dated to about 1540.

For another miniature attributable to 'Abd ul-'Aziz, see no. 16.

Inscribed

on the letter

In the name of the Ruler of All Realms! Khwaja 'Abd ul-Aziz, whose mastery is the rarity of the ages, did this portrait of the boy, Mirza-Muhammad, son of Qabahat.

عمل استاد نادر العصری خواجه عبد العزیز شبیه پسر میرزا محمد

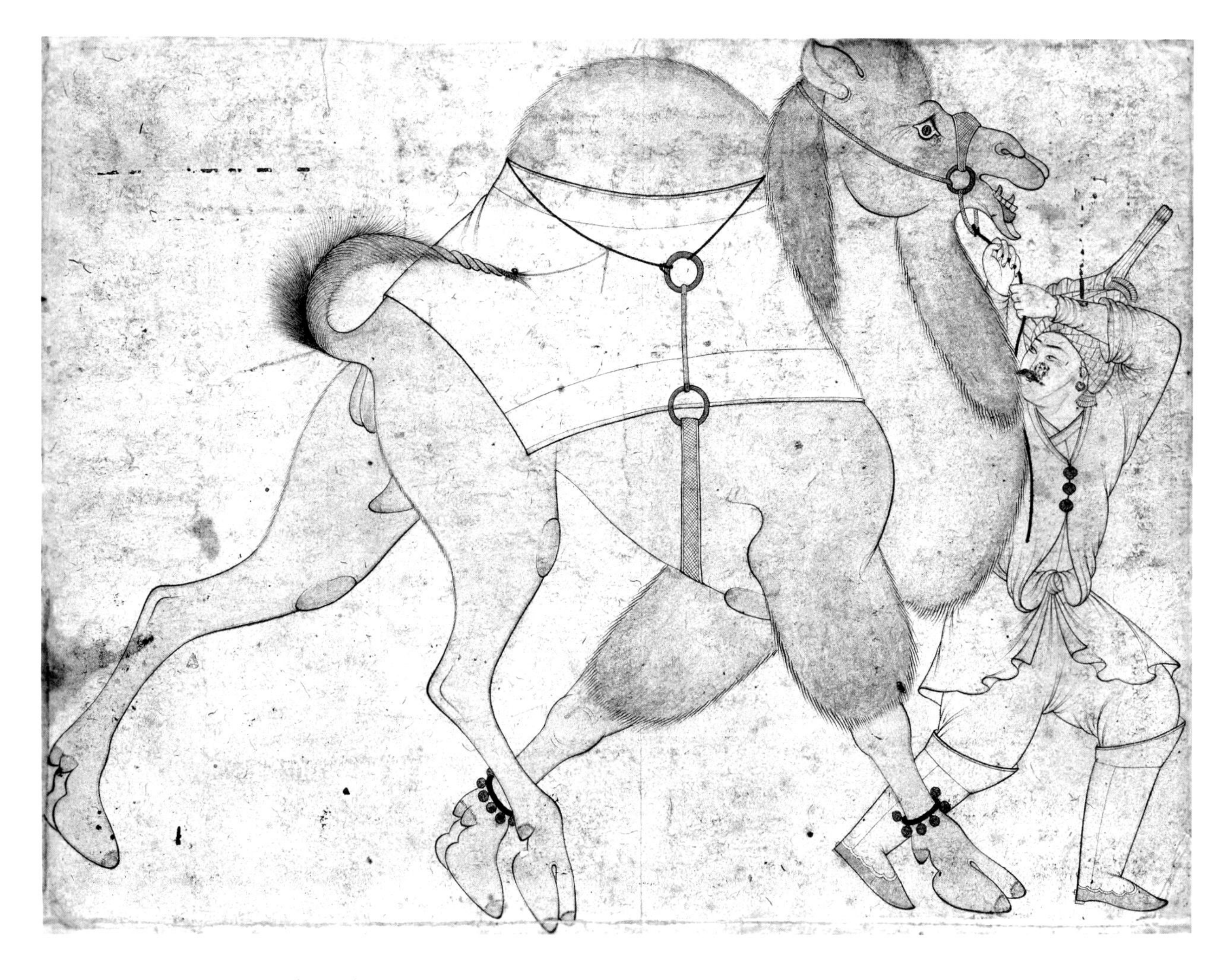

73. *Camel and Groom*

Attributable to Shaykh Muhammad

Ca. 1545
201 x 275 mm. (drawing only)
Lent by The Cleveland Museum of Art, Purchase from the Jeptha H. Wade Fund (44.489)

Line drawing in ink with brush or reed pen, was closely linked to calligraphy, an art admired by Iranians at least as much as painting. Sharp and curvilinear, with thickening and thinning forms, the strokes of this *Camel and Groom* resemble *nasta'liq* script, the style of writing favored in the sixteenth century. This boldly masterful picture can be assigned to Shaykh-Muhammad, a major draftsman and painter, who was also a notable calligrapher, as had been his father, Shaykh Kamal. Although line drawing was admired independently of painting at least as early as the fourteenth century, and artists such as Bihzad and Sultan-Muhammad were among its major exponents, Shaykh-Muhammad's spirited drawings

were eagerly sought after for inclusion in albums of calligraphies and miniatures. It could be argued that he was responsible for the surge of interest in drawing for its own sake, and that his example inspired the great Aqa-Riza (later known as Riza 'Abassi) and Sadiki Bek, whose sketches are often more admired than their paintings.

Shaykh-Muhammed never surpassed this *Camel and Groom* for linear power and purity. Although uninscribed, it can be assigned to him on many grounds, from its spirit to the appearance in it of one of the artist's most personal and oft-repeated forms, a shape resembling twisted toffee. Here, it is seen in the camel's tail; elsewhere, one finds it in sashes and turbans (see nos. 76 and 84). But there are also many other earmarks of his innovative style, ranging from the compacted proportions and overtly aggressive "military" mood, notable in the animal's stride, to the organic treatment of folds in cloth.[1]

1. For a closely related drawing, perhaps of the same camel, attributable to Mir Sayyid 'Ali, see Dickson and Welch, *The Houghton Shahnameh*, fig. 244.

74. *A Young Scribe*

By Mir Sayyid-'Ali

Ca. 1555
190 x 105 mm.
Lent by Edwin Binney, 3rd

When the second Mughal emperor, Humayun (r. 1530–1556) was exiled, he was granted sanctuary by Shah Tahmasp, who at the time was turning away from active patronage of painting. While visiting the Tabriz court in 1544, according to Qazi Ahmad, Humayun requested the services of Mir Sayyid-'Ali. "But his son," the Qazi added, "was more artful than the father," and hearing of the emperor's interest, "rushed off to India, leaving his father to follow." Bayazid's eyewitness *Memoire* on Humayun's court in exile (1540–1555) says that in 1546 he entrusted a departing Safavid envoy with an imperial rescript summoning two painters from Tabriz, Mir Sayyid-'Ali and 'Abd us-Samad. They went to Qandahar and remained there for about a year before being escorted to Kabul, where they arrived on the first of November 1549. Five years later in November 1554, they accompanied the emperor when he left for India.

Presumably the young scribe was painted soon after their arrival in India, before Humayun's death in January 1556, for it is signed "Painter of the Realm of Humayun Shahi," implying that the emperor was still alive. In style, it recalls the artist's figures in such Tabriz works as the *Nomadic Encampment* (no. 67), although the curious illogic of the book-stand perhaps hints at the artist's increasing difficulties in confronting reality.[1]

Inscribed

on top of folio of writing

On the frontispiece of his mind he had written, "Better a forceful master than a father over-kind."

at bottom

Mir Sayyid-'Ali, who is "The Rarity of the Realm of Humayun the Shah" painted this.

1. Published in color in Edwin Binney, 3rd, *Indian Miniature Painting from the Collection of Edwin Binney, 3rd* (Portland, Oregon: Portland Art Museum, 1973) p. 30.

75. *Shah Abu'l-Ma'ali*

By Dust-Muhammad

Ca. 1556–60
391 x 247 mm. (folio size)
Private Collection

Bayazid's *Memoire* says that Mulla Dust, i.e., Dust-Muhammad, "the top painter of them all," although uninvited by Emperor Humayun, joined the Mughal court at Kabul in November 1549, at the same time as Mir Sayyid-'Ali and 'Abd us-Samad. He took up service not with the emperor himself, but with Prince Kamran, Humayun's brother and dangerous rival in Afghanistan. Bayazid also supplies the motive for Mulla (more usually Master) Dust's emigration: "He could not get by without the wine the Shah [Tahmasp] had forbidden. So he left on his own and came unannounced." He also tells us that the artist was in the retinue of painters accompanying Humayun on his departure from Kabul for the reconquest of Mughal India. An uncertain Mughal source informs us that Master Dust remained in India after the succession of Humayun's son Akbar (r. 1556–1605), but that he had returned to Shah Tahmasp's court at about the age of seventy by 1560.[1]

Shah Abu'l-Ma'ali, according to Abu'l Fazl's *Akbarnama* (Story of Akbar), appeared at Humayun's court in 1551 and became, as much due to his beauty as to his audacity, a most favored protegé of the emperor. His closeness to Humayun, as well as his fanaticism and violence fomented ill feelings, especially among Humayun's sons. After Akbar's accession in 1556, Shah Abu'l-Ma'ali was strangled.

Inscribed

on folio of writing

God is the Greater. This picture is a portrait of Shah Abu'l-Ma'ali of Kashgar—he who has served as close confidant to the now late Emperor Humayun. Done by Master Dūst the Painter.

1. For a portrait of Humayun and his court of this period, attributable to Dūst-Muhammad, as well as an early seventeenth-century Mughal version of *Haftvad and the Worm* (no. 31), presumably made from a drawing or tracing brought to the Mughal court by the artist, see Ernst Kühnel and Hermann Goetz, *Indian Book Painting from Jahangir's Album in the State Library in Berlin* (London: Kegan Paul, Trench, Trubner, 1926) pls. 4, 3, and 1.

76. *Kneeling Youth Reading*

By Shaykh-Muhammad

Ca. 1555–60
155 x 083 mm. (miniature only)
Lent by the Département d'Antiquites Orientales, Section Islamique, Musée du Louvre, Paris (No. 3427)

Shaykh-Muhammad's career can be divided into three major periods: the years of apprenticeship to Master Dust-Muhammad (stylistically apparent and also supported by Qadi Ahmad) those from the late 1530s until 1556, when he was an independent master and the years from 1556 into the 1570s, when he served the Shah's nephew, Sultan Ibrahim Mirza.[1] During the middle period, his style was highly controlled, hard-edged, and comparatively austere, as can be seen from the *Camel and Groom* (no. 73). Later, under the influence of Ibrahim, as is already apparent in the present portrait, his manner became increasingly extreme, culminating in the loose, calligraphic flamboyance of the *Wayward Youths* (no. 84).

Inscribed

beneath figure
etching this is Shaykh. . . .

on folios he holds
To savor the air at the meadows—there's my desire; where she sways like a jasmined cypress—there's my desire.

1. Ibrahim Mirza was appointed governor of Mashhad in 1556 and remained there until he fell from favor in 1564. From 1564 until 1556, he was in exile in Qayin; and the bleak period of his life continued at Sabzavar from 1566 to 1574, when he was forgiven by his uncle and invited to return to court at Qazvin.

77. *An Amir Seated Beneath a Tree*

Attributable to Shaykh-Muhammad

Ca. 1557
265 x 160 mm. (miniature only)
Lent by the Museum of Fine Arts, Boston, Francis Bartlett Donation of 1912 and Picture Fund (14.592)

Bristling with sword, mace, bow, and arrows this Uzbek dates from Shaykh-Muhammad's early maturity, before he had been strongly influenced by the extremism of Sultan Ibrahim and his Mashhad court. Something of a specialist in battle scenes, of which he painted several for the Freer Jami manuscript,[1] Shaykh-Muhammad apparently respected and sympathized with this well armed figure, whose suspicious, cautious eyes kept watch on the artist. The smiling mouth pulls up slightly at the left, suggesting the sitter's—and artist's—cynical alertness. Although this Uzbek can probably be identified as one of the refugee khans who passed peacefully through Mashhad on the way to the Shah's court in 1557, he was nonetheless one of the enemy threatening the Safavid's eastern border. Neither the khan nor Shaykh-Muhammad could have overlooked the ominous symbolism of the powerful, forked trunk of the blossoming tree in the background, which a few quick hacks of a blade could have made into a cangue or yoke, the traditional restraint for prisoners.

The importance of this psychologically penetrating likeness is underscored by the treatment in relief of turban and hands.

1. See Welch, *Persian Painting*, pl. 39.

78. *Youth with A Golden Pillow*

Attributable to Mirza'Ali

Ca. 1560
176 x 101 mm. (miniature only)
Lent by the Fogg Art Museum, Gift of John Goelet, formerly in the Collection of Louis J. Cartier (1958.61)

Feline and languorous, this young man introduces us to the world of the Freer Jami of 1556–1565, a manuscript we are unable to exhibit, but whose character we can grasp from several closely related miniatures (nos. 76, 77, 79, and 80) and three illustrations in our Introduction (figs. 9–11). It was illustrated for Prince Ibrahim Mirza, nephew and son-in-law of Shah Tahmasp and son of Bahram Mirza, who became the principal patron of the court artists when Tahmasp's interest in painting declined. In mood, the Jami *Haft Awrang* differs greatly from the *Khamsa*. Gradually disappearing are the courtly, restrained manners of the 1540s, which are replaced by increasingly louche behavior, similar, perhaps, to the shift in mood in our own era from the 1950s to the 1960s.

Mirza-'Ali's princess (see no. 70) exemplifies the ethos of the 1540s in contrast to this youth, who could almost be her son. She is straight-backed and dignified, with her weight centered and her warm nature held in check—her reserve comparable to Shah Tahmasp's deepening circumspection and orthodoxy. The youth, on the other hand, seems akin to the charmingly wayward Prince Ibrahim as he sprawls, caressing the golden pillow and imagining some absent beloved. His attenuated cone-shaped neck and lithe torso are similar to those of the princess and of many of Mirza-'Ali's figures for the *Quintet* (such as no. 59). Patterns of behavior and art styles change, it seems, but not feelings. However "classic" Mirza-'Ali's earlier pictures might seem, and however mannered his later ones, all reveal the same preoccupation with human quirks and with anatomical engineering.[1]

1. For a color reproduction, see Stuart Cary Welch, "Pictures from the Hindu and Muslim Worlds," *Apollo* 107 (1978): p. 423, pl. IX.

79. *Horseman and Groom*

Attributable to Qadimi

Ca. 1560

244 x 180 mm. (miniature only)

Lent by the Fogg Art Museum, Gift of John Goelet, formerly in the Collection of Louis J. Cartier (1958.62)

Qadimi, rough and ready, appealed to young Shah Tahmasp during the years of the *Shahnama*. But the artist's Rabelaisian gusto was ill-suited to the refined ambiance of the *Quintet*, and his buoyant spirits must have been sadly dashed by being excluded from the project. Nevertheless, he lived on like some stout old housefly surviving into springtime until, at last, his talents were again in demand. Sultan Ibrahim Mirza's youthful zest for low comedy led him to include several miniatures ascribable to the aging buffoon of the workshop in his spritely Jami.[1] These pictures, outwardly far more suave and tidy than those Qadimi contributed to the *Shahnama* (nos. 17 and 23), bring to mind a burlesque comedian attired for a royal wedding. However fine the brushwork and complex the designs, their artist's coarse fun bursts through, earthy as ever. As in the *Shahnama*, his ungainly horses seemingly eye the world through goggles; mouths are disarmingly askew, as though slapped on in lipstick by the court whore, and the same old jokes are replayed for a final laugh. Once again, Qadimi rumples our sense of decorum with his exhibitionistic div, whose gambols evoke recollections of Greek satyrs and Callot's Cucurucu in the *comedia del arte*.[2]

Also ascribable to Qadimi working for Sultan Ibrahim is this sumptuously outfitted prince—the patron himself?—riding a swan-like steed, whose proportions suggest cousinship to the Ugly Duckling. Despite all the finely worked gold, elegantly up-to-date caparison and grandiose tailoring, the waggish artist's hand is unmistakable.

1. See Welch, *Persian Painting*, pl. 38 and figs. K, R, W.

2. See Dickson and Welch, *The Houghton Shahnameh*, pl. 135, fig. 265; and Welch, *Persian Painting*, fig. R.

80. *A Puzzling Amir of Bukhara*

Attributable to Shaykh-Muhammad

Ca. 1564
166 x 095 mm. (miniature only)
Private Collection

Another Uzbek visit to Mashhad occurred in 1564, towards the end of Sultan Ibrahim's governorship. A comparison of this portrait of one of the guests with another of 1557 assignable to the same artist (no. 77) helps define the changes of style under Ibrahim's patronage. The first picture is hard-edged and restrained, similar in line and spirit to the *Camel and Groom* (no. 73) of about 1545, and to the artist's earlier pictures for the Freer manuscript (such as fig. 9). The second portrait, of a piece with Shaykh-Muhammad's later contributions to the manuscript (fig. 10), has become excessive both in line and color. Although the sitters' faces closely resemble each other, here the amir has been portrayed far less tactfully. Features that seemed prestigiously stout are now fat to a point barely short of grossness, and the look of cynical caution in the first portrait now verges on petulance. Rhythms, too, have become wilder, as though a sudden storm (Ibrahim Mirza) had whipped a slightly choppy pond into sinuous turbulence. Ambiguities abound. Foliage seethes. Although both turbans are in relief, the impasto of the later one exudes the energy of a Neopolitan wedding cake. The organic wriggle of the sleeves is almost intestinal.

Though now faded, the palette of the earlier portrait was disciplined in its whites, grays, subdued yellows, flesh tones, and blues. In the second, again paralleling the changes of ethos also notable in the Jami, colors range from inky blacks to biting yellows, rich blues, mauve, and khaki green, heightened with accents of reddish orange, all inventively contained within a black ink and silver inner border. The effect is unsettling.

81. *Mir Musavvir Offers a Petition*

By Mir Sayyid-'Ali

Ca. 1565
120 x 110 mm. (folio size)
Lent by the Musée Guimet, Paris, on extended loan from the Musée du Louvre (3.619I,b)

Approximately fifteen years after painting the portrait of a young scribe for Emperor Humayun, Mir Sayyid-'Ali prepared this clever "hint" for another patron, presumably Emperor Akbar. Outwardly it is a straightforward portrait of the artist's aged father, humbly presenting a scroll, but, in fact, the offering is a lengthy petition requesting increased favors for the painter. This portrait is the only example here in which Akbar's new synthesized Mughal style predominates. If the outline and pose stem from the artist's Tabriz period, and still echo the lessons of Aqa-Mirak, the matter-of-fact realism of the old gentleman's face, tilted spectacles, and stringy Mughal turban is new. Also new are the comparative coarseness and dullness of the pigments, which might have been intended to underscore the artist's poverty, but more likely resulted from the temporary shortage of such minerals as lapis lazuli in Akbar's greatly expanding Mughal studios.

In contrast to 'Abd us-Samad, who prospered into the 1590s at the Mughal court, Mir Sayyid-'Ali, after serving in Akbar's ateliers until about 1572, then left for Mecca, never to return. Apparently, his over-sensitive, troubled spirit was not soothed by changes of scene and patronage.

Inscribed

on scroll

Exalted be He the Lord! The petition of this long-serving, this son of mine, so faithful in his service, lo these many years, is hopeful. . . . that your favors. . . . and will not be stinted. It is the hope. . . . as well of your humble servant. . . . that before too long. . . . with the matter of precedence overlooked, he may join your entourage. God grant that the shadow of the sun be. . . . !

82. *Flirtatious Lovers*

Attributable to Mirza-'Ali

Ca. 1565–70
206 x 148 mm. (miniature only)
Lent by the Museum of Fine Arts, Boston, Francis Bartlett Donation of 1912 and Picture Fund (14.595)

More extreme in stylization than the *Youth with a Golden Pillow* (no. 78) this later portrait group reflects the mood of Sultan Ibrahim Mirza during the bleak years when he was out of favor with the Shah, a time spent in dalliance as well as performing acts of piety, associating with goodly dervishes, and writing sad poetry. Despite the modesty of his allowance from Shah Tahmasp, Ibrahim continued to support a few artists, including Shaykh-Muhammad and probably Mirza-'Ali, though they may not have served him exclusively.

The lovers were painted under the influence of Shaykh-Muhammad as is evident in their spirit as well as in the interlacing forms of belts and sashes. She is pretty rather than distinguished, exaggeratedly tall, lean, and supple, yet voluptuous, and his swelling torso and limbs bring to mind a panther. In contrast to the elevatedly formal romantic scenes painted earlier for the Shah, the relationship between these young people is overtly sexual, recalling the amorous pairs of the Freer Jami. Peering into her eyes, he tugs her coat and offers a cup of wine, while she grips his shoulder and eyes him enticingly. However different these figures at first seem from Mirza-'Ali's characterizations in the *Quintet*, their passionate natures and mannerism were already implicit, from the cone-shaped necks and undulating attenuation, to the curving finger tips. They also bring to mind the artist's double-page *Hawking Party* (no. 85).

83. A Coquette Reading

Attributable to Mirza-'Ali

Ca. 1570
203 x 104 mm. (miniature only)
Lent by the Museum of Fine Arts, Boston, Income of Bartlett Fund and Special Contribution (14.593)

Snaky tufts of fur, sensually turned torsos and hips, and smouldering looks in the eye are constants in Mirza-'Ali's later portrayals of young Safavids—qualities made palpably real by the artist's mastery of anatomy in the third dimension. This charming vamp apparently reads a letter from her lover, while holding a golden pear reminiscent of the equally surrogate pillow hugged by her male counterpart in number 78.

Over the years, the fleshliness he had restrained in the days of the *Book of Kings* and *Quintet* increasingly emerged in Mirza-'Ali's miniatures, due to the changing behavior patterns catalyzed at Sultan Ibrahim's emancipated court. Subtly painterly as always, Mirza-'Ali continued to delight in applying creamy whites, as in the headcloth here. Tantalizing arabesque-shaped meanders run riot in this picture, as in the broad silhouette of the light blue coat and tiny opening in the blouse.[1]

1. Coomaraswamy erroneously numbers this miniature 14.595. (See Bibliography.)

84. *Wayward Youths*

Attributable to Shaykh-Muhammad

Ca. 1570
161 x 078 mm (miniature only)
Lent by the Département d'Antiquités Orientales, Section Islamique, Musée du Louvre, Paris (No. 7121)

One senses sour desperation in this brilliant drawing of two adolescents, who resemble Parisian demi-mondaines of the 1890s. Their pinched, etiolated faces and ambiguous emotions symbolize Sultan Ibrahim's bleak years at Sabzavar. In relation to them, Shaykh-Muhammad's young dandies of Mashhad, such as number 76, appear boyishly innocent. The artist's stylistic transformation from the crisp restraint of the *Camel and Groom* (no. 73) and the first Amir of Bukhara (no. 77) to the increasing looseness and mannerism of the second Uzbek portrait (no. 80), has now reached a stage once dubbed "the evil style." Through these years of sweeping, if superficial, change, the artist held to certain formulae, such as his evenly twisted turbans, and the seemingly kneeless curve with which he rendered legs—a legacy from his teacher, Dust-Muhammad (see nos. 31 and 34). New, however, is the dancingly calligraphic freedom of line, with its sensitive flourishes and runs—symptomatic, perhaps, of the unflagging inner spirits of Sultan Ibrahim and his court during their years of adversity.

85. Double Page Illustration: *Hawking Party*

By Mirza-'Ali

Ca. 1575
479 x 328 mm. (each folio, with borders)
a. Left half, Lent by The Metropolitan Museum of Art, Rogers Fund, 1912 (12.223.1)
b. Right half, Lent by the Museum of Fine Arts, Boston, Francis Bartlett Donation of 1912 and Picture Fund (14.624)

This splendid double page must once have been the opening scene of a great, now dispersed manuscript.[1] It can be assigned to Mirza-'Ali towards the end of his and his patrons' lives. Following his recovery from a severe illness in 1574, Shah Tahmasp experienced a change of heart. Now mellowed, he forgave many who had suffered his ire. Sultan Ibrahim was recalled to Qazvin, where he was put in charge of the innermost circle of court. A final, happier period of patronage seems to have followed, when the uncle and nephew together encouraged artists. The *Hawking Party*, with its boldly scaled, expansive forms, and its superb borders of animals and marbleizing, combines Shah Tahmasp's continuing taste for the restrained, polished style of the *Quintet* with the mannerism of Ibrahim's Mashhad and Sabzavar pictures. Tragically this artistic flowering ended soon, in 1576, when Shah Tahmasp died in his sixty-second year. He was succeeded by Isma'il II, who had been imprisoned since 1557. One of this Shah's first acts was to order the execution of Sultan Ibrahim.

OPPOSITE PAGE: Detail of no. 85.

FOLLOWING PAGES: no. 85, recto, left, and verso, right.

1. For a color reproduction of the right half of this double page illustration, see Basil W. Robinson, *Persian Drawings from the 14th through the 19th Century* (Boston and Toronto: Little, Brown and Co., 1965) pl. 48. Also see Gray, *Persian Painting*, p. 158.

Bibliography

Abū'l-Fazl. *A'īn-i Akbarī*. Translated by H. Blochmann, revised by D.C. Phillot. Calcutta: Bibliotheca Indica, 1927–1939.

The second of two parts of a history of the reign of the Emperor Akbar by his confidant, Abū'l-Fazl; known as the *Institutions* of the realm.

Abū'l-Fazl. *Akbarnāmeh*. Translated by H. Beveridge. 3 vols. Calcutta: Bibliotheca Indica, 1897–1939.

The first of two parts of a history of the reign of the Emperor Akbar by his confidant, Abū'l-Fazl; known as the *Annals*.

Akimushkin, O. F. and A. A. Ivanov. *Persidskie miniatyuri XIV–XVII vv* [Persian Miniatures of the 14th–17th Centuries]. Moscow: Nauka, 1968.

Arnold, Sir Thomas W. *Painting in Islam: A Study of the Place of Pictorial Art in Muslim Culture*. Oxford: Oxford University Press, 1928.

Badā'ūnī. *Muntakhab ut-Tavārīkh*. Translated by G. S. A. Ranking (vol. I), W. H. Lowe (vol. II), and T. W. Haig (vol. III). 3 vols. Calcutta: Bibliotheca Indica, 1884–1925.

History of Muslim India and especially Akbar, including "Who's Who" of eminent personalities, written 1595.

Bāyazīd Bayāt. *Tazkireh-yi Humāyūn va Akbar*. Edited by M. Hidayat Hosain. Calcutta: Bibliotheca Indica, 1941.

In Persian. "Memoire" of a Safavi emigré in service of Humayun and Akbar, written in 1591.

Beach, Milo C. *Rajput Painting at Bundi and Kota*. Ascona: Artibus Asiae, 1974.

Binney, Edwin, 3rd. *Indian Miniature Painting from the Collection of Edwin Binney, 3rd*. Portland, Oregon: Portland Art Museum, 1974.

Binyon, Laurence. *The Poems of Nizami*. London: Studio, 1928.

Binyon, Laurence, J. V. S. Wilkinson, and Basil Gray. *Persian Miniature Painting*. London: Oxford University Press, 1933.

Chandra, Pramod. *The Tūtī-nāma of the Cleveland Museum of Art.* Graz: Akademische Druck und Verlagsanstalt, 1976.

Chelkowski, Peter J., and Priscilla P. Soucek. *Mirror of the Invisible World. Tales from the Khamseh of Nizami.* New York: The Metropolitan Museum of Art, 1975.

Coomaraswamy, Ananda K. *Les miniatures orientales de la collection Goloubew au Museum of Fine Arts de Boston.* Paris and Brussels: Editions G. Van Oest, 1929.

Dickson, Martin Bernard. *Shah Tahmasb and the Uzbeks.* Ph.D. dissertation, Princeton University, 1958.

Published on demand by University Microfilms, Ann Arbor, Michigan. Library of Congress Card Number: Mic. 58-7838.

Dickson, Martin Bernard and Stuart Cary Welch. *The Houghton Shahnameh.* Cambridge, Mass.: Harvard University Press, in press.

See Bibliography for additional Persian sources as well as other references.

Dūst-Muhammad. *Hālāt-i Hunaravan, or, A Treatise on Calligraphists and Miniaturists.* Edited by M. Abdullah Chaghtai. Lahore: Chabuk Sawaran, 1936.

In Persian. An edition, under the editor's titles, of the Preface to the *Bahram Mizra Album* (now in the Topkapu Sarayi Museum Library [H. 2154]). The *Album* was prepared for Prince Bahram, brother of Shah Tahmasp, and the artist Dūst-Mūhammad composed the Preface in 1544–1545.

Hafiz. *Dīvān-i Khwājeh Shams ud-Dīn Muhammad Hāfiz-i Shīrāzī.* Edited by Muhammad Qazvīnī and Qāsim Ghani. Tehrān: Kītābkhāneh-y Zavvār, 1320/1941.

In Persian. A standard edition of the *Divan* or *Collected Works* of Hafiz.

Hodgson, Marshall G. S. *The Venture of Islam: Conscience and History in a World Civilization.* 3 vols. Chicago: University of Chicago Press, 1974.

Ipsiroglu, M. S. *Siyah Qalem.* Graz: Akademische Druck und Verlagsanstalt, 1976.

Kühnel, Ernst and Hermann Goetz. *Indian Book Painting from Jahangir's Album in the State Library in Berlin.* London: Kegan Paul, Trench, Trubner, 1926.

Martin, F. R. *The Miniature Painting and Painters of Persia, India, and Turkey from the 8th to the 18th Century.* 2 vols. London: Bernard Quaritch, 1912.

Mazzaoui, Michel M. *The Origins of the Safawids: Shī'ism, Sūfism, and the Ghulāt.* Wiesbaden: Franz Steiner, 1972.

The ideological underpinnings of the Safavi state.

Munshī, Iskandar Bek. *Tārīkh-i 'ālam-ārā-yi 'Abbāsī*. Edited by Iraj Afshār. 2 vols. Tehrān: Amīr-i Kabīf, 1334–1335/1955–1956.

In Persian. History of the Safavis to the death of Shah 'Abbas, including a "Who's Who" of artists alive in 1576. For an English translation of the latter, see Arnold, *Painting in Islam*, pp. 141–144.

Ogütmen, Filiz. *Miniature Art from the XIIth to the XVIIth Century: Guide to the Miniature Section of Topkapi Sarayi*. Istanbul: Guzel Sanatlar, 1966.

Pope, Arthur Upham, Ed. *Survey of Persian Art from Prehistoric Times to the Present*. 6 vols. Oxford: Oxford University Press, 1939–1958.

Pinder-Wilson, R. H. *Paintings from the Muslim Court of India*. London: British Museum, 1976.

Qāzī Ahmad Qumi. *Gulistān-i Hunar* [The Garden of the Arts]. Edited by Ahmad Suhaylī Khwānsārī. Tehrān: Bunyād-i Farhang-i Irān, 1352/1973.

In Persian. Key Safavi "Who's Who" of artists; includes *Treatise on Calligraphy* by Sultan-'Ali of Mashhad. For an English translation of the latter, see V. Minorsky. *Calligraphers and Painters*. Washington, D.C.: Smithsonian Institution, Freer Gallery of Art, 1959.

Qazvīnī, Muhammad and Qāsim Ghani, eds. *Dīvān-i Khwājeh Shams ud-Dīn Muhammad Hāfiz-i Shīrāzī*. Tehrān: Kitābkhāneh-y Zavvār, 1320/1941.

In Persian. A standard edition of the *Divan* or *Collected Works* of Hafiz.

Robinson, Basil W. "Origin and Date of Three Famous Shah-nameh Illustrations," *Ars Orientalis* I (1954): 105–112.

Robinson, Basil W. *A Descriptive Catalogue of the Persian Paintings in the Bodleian Library*. Oxford: Clarendon Press, Oxford University Press, 1958.

Robinson, Basil W. *Persian Drawings from the 14th through the 19th Century*. Boston and Toronto: Little, Brown and Co., 1965.

Robinson, Basil W. *Persian Paintings in the India Office Library: A Descriptive Catalogue*. London: Sotheby Parke Bernet, 1976.

Robinson, Basil W. *Persian Miniature Painting from Collections in the British Isles*. London: Victoria and Albert Museum, 1967.

Robinson, Basil W., Ernst J. Grube, G. M. Meredith-Owens, R. W. Skelton, and Ivan Stchoukine. *The Keir Collection: Islamic Painting and the Arts of the Book*. London: Faber and Faber, Ltd., 1976.

Sakisian, Armenag Beg. *La Miniature persane du XIIe au XVIIe siècle*. Paris and Brussels: G. Van Oest, 1929.

Sām Mīrza. *Tuhfeh-yi Sāmī* [Some Princely Curios]. Edited by Vahid Dastgirdi. Tehrān: Armaghān, 1314/1936.

A "Who's Who" of poets, written in 1550 by Prince Sam, brother of Shah Tahmasp. For an English translation of extracts, see Mahfuz ul Haq. "Persian Painters, Illuminators, and Calligraphists, Etc.," *Journal of the Asiatic Society of Bengal*, n.s. 38 (1932): 239–249.

Schroeder, Eric. *Persian Miniatures in the Fogg Museum of Art*. Cambridge, Mass.: Harvard University Press, 1942.

Schulz, Philipp Walter. *Die persisch-islamische Miniaturmalerei: ein Beitrag zur Kunstgeschichte Irans*. 2 vols. Leipzig: Karl W. Hiersemann, 1914.

Stchoukine, Ivan V. *Les Peintures des manuscrits timurides*. Bibliothèque Archéologique et Historique, Tome LX. Paris: Institut Français d'archéologie de Beyrouth, 1954.

Stchoukine, Ivan V. *Les Peintures des manuscrits safavis de 1502 à 1587*. Bibliothèque Archéologique et Historique, Tome LXVII. Paris: Institut Français d'archéologie de Beyrouth, 1959.

Stchoukine, Ivan V. *La Peinture turque d'après les manuscrits illustres*. Bibliothèque Archéologique et Historique, Tome LXXXIV. Paris: Institut Français d'archéologie de Beyrouth, 1966.

Tahmāsb, Shāh. *Tazkireh-yi Shāh Tahmāsb*. Edited by 'Abd ush-Shukūr. Berlin: Kaviyani, 1343/1924.

In Persian. The Shah's *Memoirs*, an account of his life and reign, written c. 1562.

Titley, Norah M. *Miniatures from Persian Manuscripts: A Catalogue and Subject Index of Paintings from Persia, India, and Turkey in the British Library and the British Museum*. London: British Museum Publications, Ltd., 1977.

Togan, Zeki Velidi. *On the Miniatures in Istanbul Libraries*. Istanbul: Umumî Turk Tarihi Kürsüsü, Istanbul Edebiyat Fakült, 1963.

Welch, Anthony. *Artists for the Shah: Late Sixteenth-Century Painting at the Imperial Court of Iran*. New Haven and London: Yale University Press, 1976.

Welch, Stuart Cary. *The Art of Mughal India*. New York: The Asia Society, 1964.

Welch, Stuart Cary. *A Flower from Every Meadow*. New York: The Asia Society, 1973.

Welch, Stuart Cary. *Imperial Mughal Painting*. New York: Braziller, 1978.

Welch, Stuart Cary. *Indian Drawings and Painted Sketches*. New York: The Asia Society, 1976.

Welch, Stuart Cary. *A King's Book of Kings: The Shahnameh of Shah Tahmasp*. New York: The Metropolitan Museum of Art, 1972.

Welch, Stuart Cary. *Persian Painting: Five Royal Safavid Manuscripts of the Sixteenth Century*. New York: Braziller, 1976.

Welch, Stuart Cary. "Pictures from the Hindu and Muslim Worlds," *Apollo* 107 (1978): 423, pl. IX.

Wilkinson, J. V. S. *The Shah-Namah of Firdausi: The Book of the Persian Kings*. Introduction by Laurence Binyon. Oxford: Oxford University Press, 1931.

Woods, John E. *The Aqquyunlu: Clan, Confederation, Empire*. Minneapolis and Chicago: Bibliotheca Indica, 1976.

On the history and institutions of the White Sheep Turkman.

Zetterstéen, K. V. and C. J. Lamm. *Mohammad 'Asafī: The Story of Jamāl and Jalāl*. Uppsala: Vilhelm Ekmans Universitetsfond, 1948.

Zuka, Yahya. "Khāvarān-nāmeh: Nushkheh-yi khattī-o musavvar-i Mūzsh-yi Hunarhā-yi Tazyīnī" [The Khavaran-nameh: The Illustrated Copy in (Tehran's) Museum of Decorative Arts], *Hunar-o Mardum* 20 (1343/1964): 17–29.

Wonders of the Age

was designed by Katy Homans,

set in Monotype Dante by Michael & Winifred Bixler,

and printed on Warren's Lustro Offset Enamel by Acme Printing Company